What Every Teacher Should Know About

Diverse Learners

SECOND EDITION

Other Corwin Books by Donna Walker Tileston

Closing the Poverty and Culture Gap: Strategies to Reach Every Student, 2009

Teaching Strategies That Prepare Students for High-Stakes Tests, 2008

Teaching Strategies for Active Learning: Five Essentials for Your Teaching Plan, 2007

What Every Parent Should Know About Schools, Standards, and High Stakes Tests, 2006

Ten Best Teaching Practices: How Brain Research, Learning Styles, and Standards Define Teaching Competencies, Second Edition, 2005

Training Manual for What Every Teacher Should Know, 2005

What Every Teacher Should Know About Learning, Memory, and the Brain, 2004

What Every Teacher Should Know About Diverse Learners, 2004

What Every Teacher Should Know About Instructional Planning, 2004

What Every Teacher Should Know About Effective Teaching Strategies, 2004

What Every Teacher Should Know About Classroom Management and Discipline, 2004

What Every Teacher Should Know About Student Assessment, 2004

What Every Teacher Should Know About Special Learners, 2004

What Every Teacher Should Know About Media and Technology, 2004

What Every Teacher Should Know About the Profession and Politics of Teaching, 2004

What Every Teacher Should Know: The 10 Book Collection, 2004

Strategies for Teaching Differently: On the Block or Not, 1998

DONNA WALKER TILESTON

AlBatool Aqeel
Fall 2016

What Every Teacher Should Know About

Diverse Learners

SECOND EDITION

CORWIN
A SAGE Company

For information:

Corwin
A SAGE Company
2455 Teller Road
Thousand Oaks,
  California 91320
www.corwin.com

SAGE Pvt. Ltd.
B 1/I 1 Mohan Cooperative
  Industrial Area
Mathura Road,
  New Delhi 110 044
India

SAGE Ltd.
1 Oliver's Yard
55 City Road
London EC1Y 1SP
United Kingdom

SAGE Asia-Pacific Pte. Ltd.
33 Pekin Street #02-01
Far East Square
Singapore 048763

Printed in the United States of America

Library of Congress Cataloging-in-Publication Data

Tileston, Donna Walker.
What every teacher should know about diverse learners/Donna Walker Tileston.—2nd ed.
    p. cm.
Includes bibliographical references and index.
ISBN 978-1-4129-7175-1 (pbk.)

   1. Multicultural education—United States—History. 2. Minorities—Education—United States—History. I. Title.

LC1099.3.T55 2010
370.117—dc22   2010004180

This book is printed on acid-free paper.

10   11   12   13   14   10   9   8   7   6   5   4   3   2   1

Acquisitions Editor:	Carol Chambers Collins
Associate Editor:	Megan Bedell
Editorial Assistant:	Sarah Bartlett
Production Editor:	Veronica Stapleton
Copy Editor:	Tomara Kafka
Typesetter:	C&M Digitals (P) Ltd.
Proofreader:	Dennis W. Webb
Indexer:	Molly Hall
Cover Designer:	Karine Hovsepian

Contents

Acknowledgments

Thanks to my editor extraordinaire, Carol Collins, for her patience and her belief in my work.

About the Author

Donna Walker Tileston, EdD, is a veteran teacher and the president of Strategic Teaching and Learning, a consulting firm that provides services to schools throughout the world. Also a prolific author, Donna's publications include *Ten Best Teaching Practices: How Brain Research, Learning Styles, and Standards Define Teaching Competencies*, Second Edition (Corwin, 2005); *Strategies for Teaching Differently: On the Block or Not* (Corwin, 1998); and *Closing the Poverty and Culture Gap: Strategies to Reach Every Student* (Corwin, 2009). This series, *What Every Teacher Should Know*, won the prestigious AEP award in 2005.

Donna received her BA from the University of North Texas, her MA from East Texas State University, and her EdD from Texas A&M University Commerce. She may be reached at www.whateveryteachershouldknow.com.

Introduction

The Supreme Court's 1954 decision in Brown versus Board of Education of Topeka, Kansas, *made equal access to public education the law of the land. With each decade we have increased the proportion of the U.S. population in school, including children from more diverse socioculture and economic backgrounds, and diversified the kinds of educational programs offered. But these accomplishments have fallen far short of the vision of a universal school system that provides all children with equal access to success in school.*

—M. C. Wang and J. A. Kovach

Since the first edition of this book in 2004, so much has happened in this country in regard to understanding culture and poverty. This book contains about 60% new information about what we must do in this century to lift children out of poverty and build a strong middle class. I know of no country in the world without a middle class that is a strong democracy. As the faces of the children rapidly change to reflect the exponential changes in our demographics, education struggles to understand the learning differences and the changes that must be put into place.

As the economy, resources, and affluence of the city have moved to the suburbs, we have been left with many large cities whose inner-city area is a myriad of crumbling buildings, graffiti, and the poor who cannot afford to leave. In the mountains, along our borders, and in the towns and counties that make up our country we find children who are poor and who often are hungry. Add to that a struggling economy and the lack of resources available, and we have an educational system that, despite its best efforts, cannot provide equal access to success. Teachers are leaving the field in droves either to enter a different field or to follow the resources to the newer suburbs of the city. Why not? Our society measures the success of schools and its personnel on test scores—often single test scores. Even when the measurement includes other factors, such as dropout rates, attendance rates, and the percentage of students taking advanced courses, the complex problems of teaching a diverse population of students from ethnic and language minority backgrounds remain a factor usually not considered. Studies by Education Trust show that working in high poverty areas will often gain teachers less money, poorer conditions, and instability (2008). Why, then, would educators choose to teach in these areas?

Throughout this book, we will examine how we got to this place and look at some of the best research available for helping to narrow and eventually close the achievement gap for minority students. While many of the solutions for schools are a matter of combining resources from state and local communities, including health and dental care, family assistance, and the collaboration of community leaders in the decision making process, this book focuses on what the classroom teacher can do to help ensure that these students learn—and learn at a high level. I have also focused on how to empower teachers so that they have the information and resources to be able to make a difference.

Brain research has afforded us insights into new ways to reach these students. We now know, for instance, that students from poverty tend to learn better when visual and kinesthetic approaches are used than they do when a traditional curriculum based on verbal teaching is employed (Payne, 2001). English language learners may not have the language acquisition skills necessary for processing a great deal of data in a verbal format.

By incorporating visual tools into the curriculum and by providing a variety of teaching strategies, we can reach these students at a level never before possible.

The Vocabulary Summary of this book contains terms often used in conjunction with working with urban learners. Form 0.1 provides a list of the vocabulary words for this book. In the space provided, write your definition of the word at this time. After you have read this book, go back to your original answers to see if you have changed your mind about your definitions.

In addition, I am providing a pretest to help you identify your own knowledge of the vocabulary that will be used in this volume. At the end of the book are a posttest and the answers to the test for your self-assessment.

Form 0.1 Vocabulary List for Diverse Learners

Vocabulary	Your Definition	Your Revised Definition
Best practices		
Bias		
Classroom climate	how the class feels its atmosfear	
Cultural identity		
Direct instruction	Clear instruction exactly what to do	
Diversity	Diferences	
English language learners	when someones main lang is not E	
Ethnicity	where are you from	
Ethnocentrism		
Exceptionality	not like othrs	
Hidden rules of society	traddihions.	
Learning environment	the place where you learn	
Locus of control		
Melting-pot theory	Diversity in one place	
Minority group and they have less #R	group that has the same features	
Modality		
Modifications	changes	
Motivation	what makes you reach your goals	
Response to intervention		
Self-efficacy فعاليَّة		
Self-esteem	how you look to yourself	
Self-talk	when you have conversation with yourslf	
Socioeconomic status		
Stereotyping	when you name a person depends on their situation	

Vocabulary Pretest

Instructions: For each question given, choose the best answer or answers. More than one answer may be correct. The answer key appears on page 89.

1. The belief that one culture is superior to other groups is called . . .
    A. The melting-pot theory
    B. Ethnocentrism
    C. Exceptionality
    D. Diversity

2. Diane Madden is a teacher at East Middle School where she teaches eighth-grade English. Ms. Madden talked with teachers from the seventh grade prior to the beginning of school and asked them to give her their opinions about the students she will be teaching this year. Several of the teachers said that she shouldn't even try to teach "those" students the classics because they will not understand them. This advice is what type of bias?
    A. Linguistic
    B. Exclusion
    C. Persuasive
    D. Stereotyping

3. Students who come from poverty are usually not . . .

   A. Kinesthetic learners
   B. Visual learners
   C. Auditory learners
   D. Declarative learners

4. Students who believe that they just have bad luck in school may be suffering from poor . . .

   A. Diversity
   B. Locus of control
   C. Self-efficacy
   D. Self-esteem

5. Students who believe that they can succeed because they have succeeded in the past are practicing . . .

   A. The auditory modality
   B. Locus of control
   C. Self-efficacy
   D. Extrinsic motivation

6. Teachers who tell students that they will get candy for good work are using . . .

   A. Locus of control
   B. Intrinsic motivation
   C. Self-fulfilling prophecy
   D. Extrinsic motivation

7. Which of the following is not true of response to intervention?

   A. It is a part of the 2004 amendments to ESEA.
   B. It is the responsibility of regular education teachers as well as special education.
   C. It allows students to be placed in special education if the learning difficulty is caused by poverty.
   D. It requires interventions before a student shows failure.

8. Students who have lived in situations of great stress over time often experience . . .

   A. Imaginary audience
   B. Self-fulfilling prophecy

C. Exceptionality

D. Learned helplessness

9. Teachers who teach in a variety of formats so that they teach to all races and ethnicities are practicing . . .

A. Contextualization

B. Ethnocentrism

C. Pluralism

D. Indirect teaching

10. English language learners (ELLs) . . .

A. Are considered to have low socioeconomic status

B. Speak a language other than English as their primary language

C. Are often shy in class

D. Have low intrinsic motivation to learn

11. Raul is in Mr. Vasquez's math class at Moors Middle School. Raul is struggling because he cannot grasp some of the math concepts being taught. Mr. Vasquez has added graphic organizers to help students like Raul learn more successfully. Raul is probably what kind of learner?

A. Kinesthetic

B. Visual

C. Auditory

D. Dual skill

12. Which of the following are used to determine at-risk students?

A. Low socioeconomic status

B. ELL status

C. Previous failure

D. Ethnicity

13. Marty came to school on Friday with red streaks in his hair (just like his two best friends). Marty is exhibiting . . .

A. Personal fable

B. Self-efficacy

C. Imaginary audience

D. Self-fulfilling prophecy

14. When students become what we expect them to become, it is called . . .

    A. An imaginary audience
    B. A self-fulfilling prophecy
    C. Self-efficacy
    D. Personal fable

15. Most students in the classroom are which type of learners?

    A. Auditory
    B. Visual
    C. Kinesthetic
    D. Intrinsic

16. *Diversity* means . . .

    A. Differences
    B. Ethnicity
    C. Exceptionality
    D. Bias

17. The belief that people moving to this country should become like us is called . . .

    A. Exceptionality
    B. Ethnocentrism
    C. Multicultural
    D. The melting-pot theory

18. Intrinsic motivation is triggered by . . .

    A. Relevance
    B. Stickers
    C. Emotions
    D. Relationships

19. Kelvin Waters has difficulty completing tasks once he begins. Research on which topic would be most helpful for him?

    A. The metacognitive system
    B. The self-system

C. The cognitive system

D. The procedural system

20. Which of the following is part of classroom climate?

A. The lighting in the room

B. The amount of tension in the room

C. The way the room smells

D. The socioeconomic status of the students

*To my brother Mark Walker, with whom I am working
to make life better for children, not just in education
but in the medical field, in the community, and in better
early childhood programs within the inner city.*

*To all the wonderful children at
the Open Door Preschool in Dallas, Texas.*

Influences

In the increasingly competitive international economy, a good education is the best—and perhaps only— insurance. This is especially true for students who are poor, English language learners, or members of minority groups. "Get a good education," we say. "It is the best chance you have."

—Carmen G. Arroyo

N o one deserves an inferior education and certainly no teacher wants to provide a watered down version of the curriculum. Carmen Arroyo (2008) says that although states say a good education is important in helping children to become successful adults, they often do not provide equitable resources or equal access to a quality education. "Despite national imagery full of high flying concepts like 'equal opportunity' and 'level playing field,' English-learner, low-income, and minority students do not get the extra school supports they need to catch up to their more advantaged peers; they all too frequently receive less than do other students" (Arroyo, p. 1). In many cases, education has failed to provide teachers with the background knowledge to appropriately teach children from cultural backgrounds outside the traditional northern European model of today's classroom. The National Task Force on Minority High Achievement says that, with the exception of Asian Americans, minority students—even those who are not poor—tend to score lower on achievement tests than whites who are poor.

We do not have much control over the environment from which our students come, nor do we have much control over some of the adversity they must overcome to be successful. What we do have control over is seven to eight hours of their lives five days a week. During that time, we can give them the hope, the dreams, and the tools to make their lives meaningful. We can give them the kind of quality education that will be necessary to be successful in this century, and we can guide them to develop resiliency toward their issues associated with poverty.

Diversity refers to differences. Today's learners are different in many ways, such as race, culture, ethnicity, socioeconomic status, gender, learning modalities, cognitive development, social development, and the rate in which they take in information and retrieve it.

Each student in the classroom is unique in some way. A successful teacher recognizes that diversity may affect learning and thus works toward a classroom in which diversity is celebrated and revered. In such a classroom there is a conscious effort to help students recognize and respect differences; there is a sense of community. In this book, we will look at how diversity affects what we do in the classroom and what we can do to make sure that there is an equal opportunity for a high quality education.

A FEW DEFINITIONS TO CONSIDER

When researching students today, it is important that, as educators, we have a common language with which to refer to the facts. To help us look at the issues involved in diverse populations, I offer two definitions to provide common ground in our discussion.

1. Ethnic Identity

   The Regional Education Lab (Brown University, 2007) reports that "one of the most basic types of identity is ethnic identity, which entails an awareness of one's membership in a social group that has a common culture. The common culture may be marked by a shared language, history, geography, and (frequently) physical characteristics" (p. 4).

2. Cultural Identity

   The Regional Education Lab (2007) identifies cultural identity as people from multiple ethnic backgrounds who may identify as belonging to the same culture. For example, in the Caribbean and South America, several ethnic groups may share broader, common Latin cultures. Social groups existing within one nation may share a common language and a broad cultural identity but have distinct ethnic identities associated with a different language and history. Ethnic groups in the United States are an example of this.

The chart below is one way to examine your own cultural identity. Language identifies us—not just through our words but also in our use of body language with the language and the way in which we use emphasis or inflection. Thus the language with which you grew up will continue to influence you regardless of the language you speak as an adult. The beliefs,

Figure 1.1   Your Cultural Identity

Your birthplace	Your first language	Your caretakers	Your friends	Your beliefs
Jeddah	Arabic			Islam

attitudes, and expectations of your caregivers and your peer groups have a tremendous impact on your own ideals and expectations. Through what kind of glasses do you view the world? That is your cultural identity.

BACK TO THE FUTURE

To understand students today, it is important to look at the recent past and some of the major influences in the world that have affected schools.

Brown versus Board of Education

Lisa Cozzens (1998), writing for Watson.org, describes the scene that led to this important legislation:

> In Topeka, Kansas, a black third-grader named Linda Brown had to walk one mile through a railroad switch-yard to get to her black elementary school, even though a white elementary school was only several blocks away. Linda's father, Oliver Brown, tried to enroll her in the white elementary school but the principal refused. Brown went to McKinley Burnett, the head of Topeka's branch of the National Association for the Advancement of Colored People (NAACP) and asked for help. The NAACP was eager to assist the Browns as it had long wanted to challenge segregation in public schools. With Brown's complaint, it had the right plaintiff at the right time.

The U.S. District Court for the District of Kansas heard Brown's case from June 25–26, 1951. The argument presented in the case was that segregated schools, even when they provided the same education—by the very fact that they were separate—sent a message that black children were inferior to white children. That constituted unequal schools. In other words schools were not just about bricks and mortar but also about the messages that they sent to children socially.

The argument made by the Board of Education was that segregated schools simply prepared students for the way of life of the differing races in which they would be a part in real life. The court found in favor of the Board of Education, but they wrote: "Segregation of white and colored children in public schools has a detrimental effect upon the colored children. . . . A sense of inferiority affects the motivation of a child to learn" (Cozzens, 1998).

The ruling was challenged and made its way to the Supreme Court along with several other cases along the same lines.

On May 17, 1954, Chief Justice Earl Warren read the decision of the unanimous Court:

> We come then to the question presented: Does segregation of children in public schools solely on the basis of race, even though the physical facilities and other "tangible" factors may be equal, deprive the children of the minority group of equal educational opportunities? We believe that it does . . . We conclude that in the field of public education the doctrine of "separate but equal" has no place. Separate educational facilities are inherently unequal. Therefore, we hold that the plaintiffs and others similarly situated for whom the actions have been brought are, by reason of the segregation complained of, deprived of equal protection of the laws guaranteed by the Fourteenth Amendment. (Cozzens, 1998)

It is interesting to note that while we have moved a long way from the days of separate is equal, we have come full circle back to a way of life in the urban cities, older suburbs, and densely populated areas of the mountains, bayous, and woodlands that resembles the segregation of the 1950s. Wang and Kovach (1996) write that with increased urban sprawl, those who could afford the suburbs have moved out of the inner cities with its high crime rate, poor air quality, and decaying brick. This has left the inner cities to those who cannot leave for economic or other reasons. Inner-city students are often sent to older buildings wired well before the time of high technology. These schools often provide resources inferior to those of the new, more modern schools going up every year in the suburbs and the smaller communities outside the city. Wang and Kovach call this "residential segregation" and that with the movement of resources, jobs, and people from central city to the suburbs a hostile environment has been created for children, families, and institutions embedded in the cities, including schools.

Indeed, after more than 50 years of desegregation issues, we are still battling whether all students have equal access to a quality education. Carmen Arroyo (2008), director of research for Education Trust, states "Many states still fail to give equal funding to the school districts serving the students who face the greatest challenges." In its report on the 2004–2005 school year, Education Trust (2007) reported that schools in high poverty areas were more likely to have

1. Teachers who were either not certified educators or who were not certified in the subject that they taught

2. Teachers with less experience

3. Teachers who made, on average, $1000 less than teachers in other schools

4. A high turnover rate

A study by Bartelt (1994) looked at the relationship between micro social forces and educational accomplishment in the macro ecology of 53 major cities across the country. The study concludes with inner schools that serve populations of poverty will remain there because they are trapped due to their economic status. Inner-city schools are increasingly remnant-population schools and communities trapped by the irrelevant economic links to diminished labor markets. Because those left in the inner city are primarily minority groups, we seem to be back to the issue of equity underpinning *Brown versus Board of Education*; not just equity of buildings and resources, but of educational opportunities and outcomes as well. Williams (1996) says that urban students' achievement reflects historical, social, and economic events: the dynamics of the relocation of industry from cities to suburbs, the transition to a postindustrial service economy, the history of racial segregation, and a new wave of large scale immigration.

WHAT ARE THE ISSUES NOW?

Students today are different, not just in the colors they dye their hair, their music, or even the things they pierce; they are different in the way that they learn and process information. Today's students live in a multimedia world that is not limited by boundaries of the United States. They are more aware, more outspoken, and more demanding than past generations, and it takes a teacher with motivation and high energy to meet the challenges they produce.

The 2000 decade has already proven to be a time of great change in this country. We have become vulnerable for the first time to enemies outside our borders, we have become embroiled in war and the economy has proven fickle. For the first time in quite a while, the middle class has suffered major changes in their financial situations with the reversal in the stock market of the telecommunications industry and the loss of jobs by professionals. The chasm between the haves and the have-nots seems to have grown enormously. Middle-class families have lost their homes and those still in their homes find themselves trying to make ends meet in a struggling economy. According to a report from Project We (Greenberg, 2007), one in four students will become diabetic and one in two will get cancer in their lifetimes. These are scary statistics for this generation. Children from poverty, who are often exposed to lead poisoning, poor nutrition, and uneven health care, may be more at risk.

As Zhoa (2009) states in his book on globalization, "Education is supposed to prepare future citizens—that is, to equip them with the necessary skills, knowledge, attitudes, and perspectives to live a prosperous and happy life as well as to perform responsibilities required of them as citizens of a society" (p. 13). He goes on to say that one of the ways we predict success in life is to look at a person's success in school.

As we look at the students who come to us from poverty, it is fitting to look at what constitutes poverty today. It is not just a matter of money. Payne (2001) says that poverty is the extent to which an individual does without resources. She further defines resources as financial, emotional, mental, spiritual, physical, support systems, and relationships. For example, *financial* resources involve the ability to buy the goods and services needed to survive and more. *Support systems* mean having people who serve as backups when we are not able to purchase goods and services for ourselves. *Relationships* refer to appropriate adult behaviors that model for students what constitutes appropriate behavior.

To what extent can we, as educators, help students to obtain resources in these areas? I am convinced that the more we can do that, the greater the possibility that we can solve inner-city educational problems.

According to Education Trust (2007), among the biggest changes in school demographics over the last decade is the increase in the number of English language learners (ELL). By 2004, the ELL student population had grown to approximately 11% of all public school students nationwide. In most states with the large percentages of ELL students, the districts with the highest concentration of these students received fewer resources, such as money, than districts with lower percentages. In Nevada and Texas, those funding gaps exceeded $1000 per student per year.

The U.S. Bureau of Statistics projects that by 2024 the majority of students in public schools will be Hispanic with African American students second and northern European students third. By 2042, the United States adult population will mirror these ethnic identities.

It is interesting to note here that one of the original arguments for equal access to education was that education should prepare students socially and through experience to live in the real world within their ethnic and cultural groups. On June 25–26, 1951, as the U.S. District Court for the District of Kansas heard Brown's case, the NAACP made the argument that segregated schools send a message that the minority (in this case black) population is inferior to the dominant population. Their expert witness, Dr. Hugh W. Speer, testified:

> If the colored children are denied the experience in school of associating with white children, who represent 90% of our national society in which these colored children must live, then the colored child's curriculum is being greatly curtailed. The Topeka curriculum or any school curriculum cannot be equal under segregation. (Cozzens, 1998)

How much more complicated this becomes as we understand that we must provide a quality education for these students who are quickly becoming the majority in America. They will be our teachers, our doctors, our professionals, and our caregivers of the immediate future. We must provide a quality education because (1) it is morally right and (2) the future of our country depends on it. We must start early; if we are going to close gaps in achievement, we must look at early childhood programs. In a study from Rand, Lynn Karoly (2007), a Rand economist who heads the California Preschool Study project, states that the project is intended to examine the role improved early childhood education may play in closing the gap by better preparing children to succeed in school. This same study found in 2007 that three of five third graders did not achieve proficiency in English-language arts, while two of five students in the same grade did not achieve proficiency in mathematics. The report states, "Those averages mask substantial differences between groups of students based on their demographic and family background characteristics. Among children in kindergarten through third grade, students who are English language learners and students whose parents did not graduate from high school are the groups most likely to fall short of proficiency standards and lack recommended school readiness skills." In addition, the study found that almost 70% of these students did not meet second grade level proficiency standards in English language arts and 85% did not meet the standards for third grade. The targeted groups that did not meet proficiency were made up largely from Hispanic, African American, and economically disadvantaged subgroups.

In the 2007 STAR test results, according to California State Superintendent of Public Instruction Jack O'Connell, it was pointed out that even when poverty is not a factor, the performance of black and Latino students is behind those of white children (Mangaliman, 2007). California's STAR test results show that African Americans and Latinos who are not poor perform at lower levels in math than white students who are poor. O'Connell notes that "these are not just economic gaps, they are racial achievement gaps." In other words, simply trying to explain away the differences in test scores between Hispanics and whites or African Americans and whites as the fault of poverty no longer holds true. Past methods of remediation did not account for the ways that so many of our schools are structured primarily to teach white students.

Changes in Identifying
Students With Learning Disabilities

Schools all over the country are building models for identifying students with learning disabilities through response to intervention. For the first time, both regular education teachers and special education teachers are jointly responsible for identifying and implementing research-based practices to determine the level of response needed by children who are struggling. No longer do we wait until a child has failed to administer instructional changes and to track their responses. Intervention is at the first sign of difficulty.

Since the passage of Education of all Handicapped Act of 1975, Public Law 94–142, much has changed in the way that we view learning and difficulties encountered with learning. We have more research from which to draw and we have documented which practices work (best practices) and their effect on student learning. We have changed our philosophy from most children can learn to all children must learn and learn at a quality level.

Response to intervention became a formal part of the 2004 reauthorization of the Individuals with Disabilities in Education Act (IDEA) partially because of the concern that, while schools were decreasing in numbers, special education was growing exponentially, especially for students of color and from poverty. According to Hosp (2009), "The basic premise of disproportionate representation is that, all other things being similar, students from different groups should be identified for special education services in similar proportions. For example, if 6% of the Caucasian students in a given district are identified for special education, we would expect about 6% of the African-American students, 6% of the Latino/a students and 6% of any other group identified" (p. 1). The same can be said if a group is underrepresented as well. This measure is not only used when examining data on ethnicity but on other measures as well such as language proficiency, gender, culture, and so on. The tenets of IDEA 2004 provide emphasis on effective instruction that is tied to state standards and delivered by a highly qualified teacher. It also emphasizes progress monitoring to inform instruction and early intervention rather than waiting for a child to fail before providing services.

Some of the assumptions on which the new legislation is built include

- All students will be taught by highly qualified teachers.
- All students will be taught from a curriculum built on standards.
- All students will be taught by teachers who know and correctly implement best practices in the classroom.
- All students will be taught by teachers who know and correctly use modifications for culture and poverty.

If these practices are not in place, the best response to intervention (RTI) model in the world would not be expected to get results any different from the models already in place. If we are going to truly identify students who need special education services, we must take into account the modifications needed in terms of how we assess and how we modify.

2

How Are We Diverse?

Diversity refers to our differences. There are many differences among students within one classroom, much more within a school. In this global society, it is not unusual to find a school in which there are as many as 30 different languages spoken and in which there is a vast difference among students in terms of socioeconomic standing. In Chapter 1, I listed an important difference among our students in terms of the ability to obtain the goods and services (resources) necessary for success. For the purposes of this chapter, we will look at the following differences:

- Differences in cultures
- Differences in learning styles or modalities
- Differences among socioeconomic groups in regard to how they view the resources that affect schools
- Differences in race/ethnicity

WHY IS IT IMPORTANT TO EXAMINE DIFFERENCES?

The single most important influence on the climate in the classroom is the teacher. The teacher can create a classroom where there is chaos and a general disrespect for others or a classroom where there is a sense of community and an appreciation for the gifts that everyone brings to the educational process. The responsibility is not all the teacher's, but a large part of what happens begins with the beliefs and commitment that the teacher brings to the classroom. We will talk about the importance of self-efficacy (past success and the belief that one can be successful again) on students, particularly on those from poverty, but it is also important to the teacher in a multicultural classroom. We must begin to enable these teachers through information on cultural differences and how to modify best practices based on cultural differences so that we build self-efficacy in our teachers. When we do that, we will see fewer teachers leave the field. Teachers say that they have not been given the information to be successful with students outside their own cultural group.

As we select materials for our classrooms, we must take into account the differences that usually appear in our schools. What is the ethnic identity of the class? Ethnic identity refers to our identity in a group in which we have a common culture based on language, history, geography, and often physical characteristics. Our materials and books should reflect that identity by using pictures, illustrations, and quotations that bridge the ethnicities. Materials and other resources should appeal to both genders, and, as teachers, we should be sure that students are called on equally. As a matter of fact, "wait time" has an effect size of 44% when it is implemented consistently and correctly (Tileston & Darling, 2009). I was once observing in a middle school science classroom in which the teacher only called on the male students to answer questions. The underlying message was that science was for boys. The skewed results from the numbers of minority and poor students in special education as learning disabled would lead us to believe that perhaps the fault is with a system built on northern European models does not correctly address the learning styles of children who are not from the majority culture.

The most important step in working with a diverse classroom is for the teacher to first examine his or her own attitudes about differences. McCune, Stephens, and Lowe (1999) recommend that teachers make a positive effort to avoid expectations of their students based on stereotypes of the culture from which they come. To meet this challenge, teachers can begin by developing good teacher-student relationships. In the northern European culture of most classrooms, substance comes first, then teachers build a relationship as they can. In most other cultures, including African American, Mexican American, and Native American, the relationship must be built first, then the substance can be taught. Teachers need to develop an awareness of practices common in various cultures, so that when children behave in a manner consistent with their culture, the behavior will not be misinterpreted. Nevertheless, teachers should discuss with students that some behaviors are acceptable at home but not at school. For example, in the African American culture, students learn by doing and they tend to be kinesthetic; a classroom in which they are expected to sit and take notes will be very difficult for them—and for the teacher as well. Our brain builds patterns from birth (or before) and if the pattern for learning has been hands-on since birth, it will take a great deal of time and effort to change that pattern— and the student has to be willing. It is far better for us as educators to change the way that we teach.

> The first common element to effective teachers in urban schools is their belief that all students can be successful learners and their communication of this belief to students. (Zeichner, 2003, p. 99)

CULTURAL DIVERSITY

Culture is the way we view the world, and it is based on shared traditions such as history, language, religion, customs, literary traditions, and rules for behavior. "Culture is dynamic and ever changing; a group's culture includes the goals, ideals, and beliefs that will ensure the group's survival. However, there are variations among individual members of a cultural group in terms of their beliefs and values" (LAB at Brown University, 2007, Part 2, p. 1). Students' experiences and prior knowledge based on their culture are part of what we call their "cultural capital."

Lindsey, Robbins, and Terrell (2009) provide the guiding principles of cultural proficiency as follows:

1. Culture is a predominant force.

2. People are served in varying degrees by the dominant culture.

3. People have individual and group identities.

4. Diversity within cultures is vast and significant.

5. Each cultural group has unique cultural needs.

6. The best of both worlds enhances the capacity of all.

7. The family, as defined by each culture, is the primary system of support in the education of children.

8. School systems must recognize that marginalized populations have to be at least bicultural and that this status creates a distinct set of issues to which the system must be equipped to respond.

9. Inherent in cross-cultural interactions are dynamics that must be acknowledged, adjusted to, and accepted.

DIVERSITY OF MODALITIES

Sousa (1995) defines modalities as three types of learning styles. While students can learn in any of the three styles, most have a learning preference or style that comes easier for them. This is especially important when working with students who are experiencing difficulty learning. If we teach and reteach using the same learning style that is not compatible with a student's mode of learning, the chances are that we will not reach that student.

Different learning styles and modality preferences tend to run in various ethnic and cultural groups. For example, students from the inner city tend to be more hands-on, kinesthetic learners.

This reflects the culture from which they come, which relies on learning by doing. In contrast, there are cultures (particularly some Eastern cultures) in which students learn by listening. A teacher who will be successful with students in urban schools where there is a mixture of cultures will use various tactics for teaching that include a variety of resources. Such a teacher does not rely on only one modality or tactic for teaching, but provides information in a variety of contexts. As Zeichner (2003) says, successful teachers "focus instruction, guiding students to create meaning about content in an interactive, collaborative learning environment" and "provide a scaffolding that links the academically challenging and inclusive curriculum to cultural resources that students bring to school" (p. 63).

Society tends to identify intelligence by looking only at those who can take in information quickly, process it efficiently, and retrieve it from long-term memory when needed. Sprenger (2002) notes that students who take in information slowly but retrieve it quickly are usually labeled as overachievers. Students who take in information quickly but retrieve it slowly are often labeled as underachievers.

In order for us to store and use information, that information must have meaning, and meaning is closely related to the way in which we take in information. If we would narrow and close the achievement barriers forever, we must pay attention to the ways in which we can help various cultures and ethnicities that have not been successful in the past make better use of the systems that control the intake, processing, and retrieval of information. Let's begin with the way that we take in information: Being able to take information in quickly and efficiently is tied to several factors, among them the learning modalities. The three modalities most often used in the classroom are auditory, visual, and kinesthetic.

Auditory Learners

The modality least used by students is auditory. Auditory learners are those who remember best information that they hear (Tileston, 2000). These students make up 20% or less of the classroom. They like lecture, adapt well to it, and tend to be successful in our traditional schools. Some other characteristics of auditory learners, according to McCune, Stephens, and Lowe (1999), are that they

- Like to talk and enjoy activities in which they can talk to their peers or give their opinions
- Encourage people to laugh
- Are good storytellers
- May show signs of hyperactivity or poor fine motor skills
- Usually like listening activities
- Can memorize easily

It is important to note that even auditory learners cannot listen to lecture all day, every day without problems. They need opportunities to talk about the information and to share their ideas so that the information becomes personally meaningful to them. The work of Sousa (1995) shows that adult learners tend to fade out mentally after about 15 minutes of lecture only to fade back in after 10 minutes of "down time." If you have ever been in a meeting that was being presented by lecture you may have noticed this happening, even though the topic might have been one of interest to you.

For students, we normally calculate the amount of time that they can listen at one time by their age. In other words, students who are nine years old will listen for about nine minutes before they fade out. Teachers who enjoy lecture can still lecture if they learn to break up the lecture into manageable chunks of time. Talk to your class for 10 minutes, and then have them do something with the information before going back to another chunk of lecture. The activity may be as simple as having the students talk to each other about what you have just said or it might be a guided practice activity. The point is to keep their brains actively involved in the learning. Ideas for meeting the needs of auditory learners include the following:

- Direct instruction, in which the teacher guides the learning through the application of declarative (what students need to know) and procedural (what students can do with the learning) objectives
- Peer tutoring, in which students help each other practice the learning
- Activities that incorporate music
- Group discussions, brainstorming, and Socratic seminars
- Specific oral directions
- Verbalizing while learning, including the use of self-talk by the teacher and the learner
- Cooperative learning activities that provide for student interaction; because cooperative learning also includes movement, more students benefit from its use

Visual Learners

The largest group in the classroom are the visual learners (Jensen, 1997). Visual learners need to see the information and to understand how things work. We could probably raise math scores all over the country today if we could find more ways to help these students *see* how math works. For visual students, drawing the problem or using nonlinguistic organizers, such as mind maps, helps them to see the problem or issue. For these learners, the axiom "I'll believe it when I see it" is absolutely true.

Use visuals often in your teaching and help students to develop mental models by using a variety of nonlinguistic organizers. Examples of nonlinguistic organizers include concept maps, fish bones, mind maps, and prediction trees. *What Every Teacher Should Know About Effective Teaching Strategies* (Tileston, 2004a) provides numerous examples of nonlinguistic organizers: For that reason, I am only including one example here. Figure 2.1 is an example of a concept map for science class. Because the brain naturally seeks patterns, these organizers employ a brain-compatible method of teaching that works for all students.

Figure 2.1   Visual Model: Mind Map

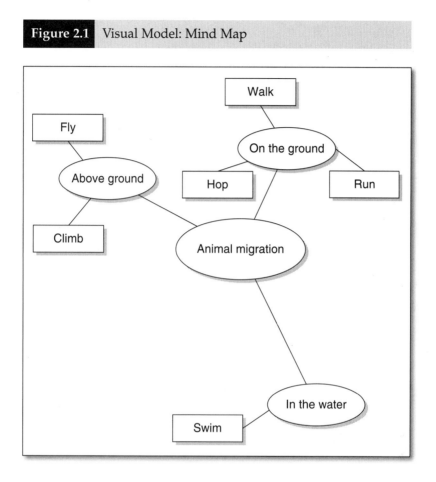

McCune et al. (1999) provide a list of some of the characteristics of visual learners. Visual learners are those who

- Have difficulty understanding oral directions
- Experience difficulty remembering names
- Enjoy looking at books or drawing pictures
- Watch the speaker's face
- Like to work puzzles
- Notice small details
- Like for the teacher to use visuals when teaching
- Like nonlinguistic organizers, because they help these students to see the information

Ideas for meeting the needs of these students include

- Using visuals when possible
- Using models, puzzles, and DVD tapes
- Demonstrating the learning, when appropriate
- Including activities in a mind-game format
- Showing patterns in the learning

Kinesthetic Learners

Kinesthetic learners are those who need movement and touching. The students in the classroom who are often off task, who tend to talk to their neighbors, and who go to the pencil sharpener or trash can at every opportunity are usually from this group of learners. These are the students who will say, "If you want me to learn how to do it, give it to me and let me work on it." They learn by doing and work well in a setting in which students work in small groups or in a classroom that incorporates such methods as discovery learning. Payne (2001) says that many urban learners fall into this category.

It is easy to see why many traditional teachers are having difficulty with these students. They need manipulatives, tactile materials, and opportunities to try things out. A wise teacher will provide opportunities for movement in the classroom and will make use of tactile materials and manipulatives whenever practical. Instead of just talking about slope in math class, combine government and math by giving students the federal guidelines for handicapped ramps and have them measure or see if the ramps around school meet the specifications. Instead of talking about World War II, take the students on a scavenger hunt to the library to find information on people, places, and battles from that era. A variety of teaching tools will go a long way toward preventing learning problems in the classroom.

Some other characteristics of kinesthetic learners, from McCune et al. (1999), are that such students

- Need opportunities to be mobile
- Want to feel, smell, and taste everything
- May want to touch their neighbors as well
- Usually have good motor skills, may be athletic
- Like to take things apart to see how they work
- May appear immature for their age group
- May be hyperactive learners

Ideas for working with these kinesthetic learners include

- Using a hands-on approach to learning
- Providing opportunities to move
- Using simulations, when appropriate
- Bringing in music, art, and manipulatives to expand the learning
- Breaking up lectures so that verbal communication by the teacher is in manageable chunks
- Providing opportunities for learning through discovery when appropriate
- Using such techniques as discussion groups or cooperative learning so that these students have an opportunity to move about and to talk with their peers

It is important to note that the greatest number of discipline problems come from this group, and a wise teacher will incorporate tools to keep this group actively involved.

Implications

It is unrealistic to think that we could meet the needs of all students for every activity, every day. The key is to provide a variety of activities. Once students are in our classrooms for a while, they learn the tricks that allow them to do minimal work. They divide up the assignments, divide up the homework, or find shortcuts in our routines. So, change up your routine; the brain likes novelty, and, by providing the learning in a variety of formats, we are more likely to teach to all students.

DIVERSITY OF SOCIOECONOMIC STATUS

Wang and Kovach (1996) argue that, while *Brown versus Board of Education of Topeka, Kansas* "made equal access to public education the law of the land," the accomplishments of the last few decades have "fallen far short of the vision of a universal school system that provides all children with equal access to success in school" (p. 17). They go on to say, "Census data from the 1990s show that the United States leads the industrialized world in numbers of children living in poverty" (p. 17). This is reflected in such legislation as the Goals 2000: Educate America Act, the School-to-Work Opportunities Act of 1994, and the reauthorization of the Elementary and Secondary Education Act as No Child Left Behind in 2001.

Yancey and Saporito (1994) found that children from inner-city neighborhoods are more likely to contract everything from measles to tuberculosis to lead poisoning. As poverty rises, both children and young adults are more likely to be crime victims, to receive inadequate health care, and to suffer from a variety of physical, psychological, and social traumas. These circumstances place children at risk of educational failure and, by necessity, place schools at the center of interconnected social problems.

While the achievement gap, as identified on standardized testing and other measures, is a national problem, it is a problem that can be solved—but the solutions need to begin early, prior to the child entering the first grade. Researchers such as Williams (1996) and Wang and Kovach (1996) remind us in the literature that the problem is not a one-stop fix but involves community support and early intervention.

Certainly the trend in the United States for all adult members of a family to work and to leave children to caregivers at day care facilities for long hours has had its toll on our nation's children. Add to that the fact that the workday has become longer, that competition for jobs is stiffer, and that we have a nation of children who do not get much one-on-one time with an adult. Kotulak (1996) has found that when caregivers talk to infants during the first three years of life the IQ levels are higher. In his study of 43 Kansas City families, he found that children who were talked to the most had "strikingly higher IQs than children whose parents didn't talk to them very much" (p. 34). Kotulak also found that "children in white-collar families hear 2,100 words per hour on an average day, compared to 1,200 words per hour in the average working-class family, and 600 words per hour in the average welfare family" (p. 34). By age four, the difference has become pronounced, with "children in welfare families having 13 million fewer words of cumulative language experience than the average child in a working-class family" (p. 34).

Jensen (1998), quoting the work of Healey, says that the evidence points to the fact that children today are not as prepared for school as they were two generations ago. He cites more children in households with fewer resources, less early motor stimulation, more exposure to drugs and medications, and fewer natural foods as the culprits. All of these factors become enlarged as we look at children from poverty. Since school readiness begins in the womb, as infants are exposed to poor nutrition, drugs, and smoking from conception, schools are seeing more and more students with learning difficulties. Jensen (2006) says that the embryo, at its peak, generates brain cells at the rate of 250,000 per minute. No wonder so many children are experiencing difficulty from birth. Moreover, he says that the relationship between an infant and its primary caretaker is important in determining whether the child develops learning problems: Since we learn much of our emotional intelligence in the first year, it is important that children be given guidance in cause-and-effect situations.

According to Payne (2001), students from poverty have predictable characteristics of which the teacher should be aware. These students live in the moment rather than planning for the long term. They will work hard for a teacher they like and may get mad or quit if they don't like the teacher. Families from poverty believe that education is important but see it as an abstract entity, whereas middle-class families value education as a means to jobs and financial stability. Families from wealthy backgrounds see education as a tradition for maintaining connections.

What Can Schools Do?

It used to be that we thought the brain was hard-wired and that it didn't change, but a new look at how the brain develops and repairs itself throughout our lives is the science of neuroplasticity. Norman Doidge (2006), in his groundbreaking book *The Brain That Changes Itself*, shows us how our brain changes throughout our lives. He tells us that we really can teach an old dog new tricks—that is those of us who have reached the age of maturity can learn new information, even change what we know, but we have to be willing. He says that the reason it is so difficult to teach us old dogs new tricks is because we have created a pattern, a paradigm in our brains and we are reluctant to change that. "As we age and plasticity declines, it becomes increasingly difficult for us to change in response to the world, even if we want to. We find familiar types of stimulation pleasurable; we seek out like-minded individuals to associate with, and research shows we tend to ignore or forget, or attempt to discredit, information that does not match our beliefs or perception of the world because it is very distressing and difficult to think and perceive in unfamiliar ways" (p. 304).

Marzano (1998), working with the research at Mid-continent Regional Educational Laboratory, says that certain teaching strategies, such as helping students to link new information to information they already know or providing specific feedback often to students as they work, can make a dramatic difference in student success: Just saying "good job" is not enough. Feedback should be diagnostic and prescriptive, should be given often, and should be sincere. As a matter of fact, telling students that they did a good job when they know that they did not do their best work may have a negative effect on the students' learning.

As teachers, we can ensure that our classrooms have the kind of environment that is conducive to feeding the brain. Jensen (1997) advises that, as educators,

We can most influence the "nurture" aspect of students. Because of that, we must follow a cardinal rule when it comes to appreciating how the brain reacts to certain influences: Start by removing threats from the learning environment. No matter how excited you are about adding positives to the environment, first work to eliminate the negatives. Those include embarrassment, finger-pointing, unrealistic deadlines, forcing kids to stay after school, humiliation, sarcasm, a lack of resources, or simply being bullied. There is no evidence that threats are an effective way to meet long-term academic goals. (p. 80)

In addition, as educators, we should be proactive in our schools' efforts to provide free breakfast and lunch to those who need it. Older students are reluctant to use the program for fear of embarrassment: Help your school find ways to make the program anonymous for students who go through the lunch line. Be familiar with community resources that provide health care and dental and eye exams to those who cannot afford them and/or cannot afford insurance. Be proactive in helping to bring resources to your students and their parents by working with social, government, and community resources and with the leaders within the community.

DIVERSITY OF RACE/ETHNICITY

There are so many differences in terms of race and ethnicity that space does not permit describing the variety within our schools. The United States has become a nation of people from all parts of the world. It is not unusual to find 30 or more languages spoken in a new kindergarten group, and it is not unusual to find classrooms that reflect the vast differences found in the communities of this country. As Gibbs (1994) reminds us that the melting pot theory, which worked well for a new nation trying to put together people from all over the world into one nation, no longer holds true for a world in which we are trying to remove the barriers of conflict, prejudice, and unequal opportunity.

Rather than trying to produce a melting pot in which everyone is alike, we must try to understand the cultures from which our students come and respect the differences. As teachers we must first examine our own values and prejudices and how those affect our students. We must then help our students to respect one another and to accept the differences. When teaching about multicultural differences, it is also important that we look beyond the obvious diversity of food, climate, and dress to the things that truly make a difference. Indeed, we must move away from a deficit theory that says children of cultures outside the dominant culture need to be "fixed" to be more like the dominant culture to an attitude that looks at their gifts first. The LAB at Brown University (2007) says

> Deficit theories about the abilities and academic achievement of culturally and linguistically diverse students suggest they do poorly in school because they lack intelligence or the right kind of background. When teachers and administrators evaluate through the lens of the dominant culture, they often cannot recognize the abilities and potential of certain groups of children. The knowledge, skills, attitudes, and values that these children bring to school are often in conflict with those valued by the school. In other words, what they know, what they can do, their world view, and their priorities do not match what the school wants them to do, how it wants them to view the world, and what its priorities are. (p. 63)

As teachers, we want to make a difference in our students' lives. Many years of research have told us that one of the most important things that we can do to reach our students is to create a relationship. As a matter of fact, in some cultures, we will not be able to do much *until* we create that relationship. Being cognizant of the communities from which our students come—and the backgrounds of those communities—is important in how we approach those relationships. To do this takes time, but my friends who work with students from various backgrounds will tell you that you gain more time in the classroom once these relationships are established. The time you invest in creating a connection is worth it because the kids are worth it.

3

Recognizing the
Signs of Bias

I n 1994, Gibbs introduced six categories of bias, and while there have been additions over time to the list, it is worth re-examining in light of what we know today. He lists six types of bias to avoid in the classroom if we are going to truly respect and celebrate diversity among students: linguistic bias, stereotyping, exclusion, unreality, selectivity, and isolation. Using his terminology for the types of bias, let's look at what the implications are for the classroom.

LINGUISTIC BIAS

Linguistic bias includes any language that is dehumanizing or denies the existence of a certain group, such as females or males. It occurs when we teach history without acknowledging the contributions of minorities. Linguistic bias also occurs when a student's name is laughed at or deliberately mispronounced. Students who have difficulty with the English language or who have not mastered proper grammar may also experience linguistic bias when others snigger or belittle them.

As a matter of fact, students new to this country often will not participate in class or answer teacher questions for fear of being ridiculed for their lack of English skills. Students may use what Payne (2001) calls *casual register*—the language they use outside of school or the way they talk—in the classroom or for writing papers instead of using proper grammar or formal register. Students who talk using Ebonics also come under this category.

These students need to know that formal register is important to use in the classroom because it helps prepare them to be successful in the outside world where use of formal register is the norm. You might have them write first in casual register and then translate it into formal register. Payne (2001) explains that, for students from poverty, language is in casual register because, for them, language is about survival. She goes on to explain that, for the middle class (around which schools are based), language is in formal register because it is about negotiation; for the wealthy, language is also in the formal register because, for them, language is about networking. Language helps define who we are; our culture usually has a common language that is not just words but is tied into our history, our beliefs, and our geography. I have two friends from France who tell each other jokes in French and laugh and laugh. When I have them tell me the jokes in English, the humor may be cute but not the knee slapping kind that my friends seem to think. When I commented on this, they explained that the jokes are funnier in French because they are wrapped around how the French view the world, or men, or life in general—depending on the joke. That is absolutely true about jokes in English as well—there are implied bits of information in most jokes. This does not apply just to jokes but to our communication with each other as well.

As teachers we can minimize linguistic bias by setting the example and by not allowing put-downs in the classroom. We will want to discuss with our classes why it is important to treat others with respect. Our students are part of a very global world, and their roles as adults will not be limited by ocean boundaries. Directly teaching students about cultural differences and how to work with other people is teaching a real-world skill. In Daniel

Pink's (2007) book *A Whole New Mind,* Pink says that in this century it will be important to be able to listen to others and realize where they are coming from even when we don't agree with them. Students need to be directly taught how to listen and how to show empathy whether they agree or not. Our students will compete in a global market, and they will have to work with our enemies as well as our friends.

STEREOTYPING

The second type of bias that we should avoid is stereotyping. This is often carried out in regard to male and female gender roles and to ethnic minorities. Encourage both male and female students to explore a wide range of activities and vocations, not just those traditionally open to men or women. For example, women today can be nurses and teachers, but they can also be attorneys and physicians if they choose. We also need to allow all students to demonstrate a variety of emotions. The LAB at Brown University (2007) took the work of earlier researchers Garcia (1994) and Geertz (1973) on culture and expanded it to show that culture is made up of "invisible webs composed of values beliefs, ideas about appropriate behavior and socially constructed truths" (p. 5). We refer to the webs as invisible because we tend to go on about our lives without consciously thinking about how we view the world. It is only when we encounter a culture that is different from our own that we become conscious of the differences. We might say, "I don't know why *they* do that" or "I don't understand why *they* said that." *They* represent people who have a set of beliefs that manifest themselves in ways different from our own. Our own culture is often hidden from us, and we frequently describe it as "the way things are." Nonetheless, one's beliefs and actions are not any more natural or biologically predetermined than any other group's set of beliefs and actions; they have emerged from the ways one's own group has dealt with and interpreted the particular conditions it has faced. In addition, culture is not fixed or static but is constantly changing. Stereotypes about culture do not hold up because, first, culture changes with time, and second, we pick and choose from our culture those values and ideas that we want and so none of us are exactly alike.

When we select materials and books, we need to be cognizant of those that show minorities in the same kind of roles that would be shown for other students. For example, minorities perform leadership roles, job-related roles, and family roles, just as other segments of the population do. Help students to know that they have many choices in life, and they are not limited by ethnicity, race, religion, or gender.

Jensen (2010) talks about a condition called "resigned learner" or learned helplessness (LH). "When there is a failure to avoid or escape an unpleasant or aversive stimulus that occurs as a result of previous exposure to unavoidable, painful stimuli, it is referred to as LH. Individuals with LH believe that no matter what they do, they can't succeed; thus, a pattern of passivity and withdrawal occurs, and the recognition that potential solutions exist is totally lost. Once acute helplessness is experienced in an area of their life, transference to other areas is common. This expectation of failure, if not reversed, eventually interferes with learning, achievement, and, ultimately, success in life" (p. 31). As teachers we strive to help students feel that they do have control over their success in school, and we make a conscious effort to help them see the relationship between what they do and their success. Students from poverty often believe that they do not have control over their lives and that outside forces such as *luck* control what happens to them. It is important that as educators we have high expectations for all of our students. McKinney, Flenner, Frazier, and Abrams (2006) suggest that urban children are likely to be victims of labels that communicate and foster low expectations. I have never met a teacher who intended to have low expectations for students, but misconceptions about children from poverty may cause educators to believe that they are children who need to be "fixed" rather than looking at them as children who have different experiences. According to Zeichner (2003), "Research clearly shows that teacher education students tend to view diversity of student background as a problem, rather than as a resource that enriches teaching and learning. Moreover, many of these future teachers have negative attitudes about racial, ethnic, and language groups other than their own. Such attitudes manifest as low expectations, which are then expressed in watered down and fragmented curriculum for children of poverty and diverse cultures" (p. 100).

Payne (2001) has identified one trait often found in students from poverty: they feel a sense of hopelessness and lack of control over their circumstances. We are not born with this trait; it is acquired through our environment. When students believe they have no control over their lives or their circumstances, they are more likely to drop out mentally, to be unmotivated, and to become depressed or even discipline problems. As teachers we have the power to give them hope and to give them some control over the circumstances in our classrooms. Allow students to help shape the rules or norms for your classroom, ask their opinions and advice on issues, and give them opportunities to reflect on and evaluate their own learning. Jensen (1997) says, "Our brain generates different chemicals when we feel optimistic and in control. These endorphins ensure pleasure, the 'flow state' and intrinsic motivation" (p. 39).

EXCLUSION

The third type of bias to avoid is exclusion. Exclusion is simply the lack of representation by a group. It can also be the removal of a group from the larger group based on race, ethnicity, religion, or gender. A science teacher calling only on male students to answer questions or identifying minority students for special education testing simply because they do not learn in the way that the dominant culture learns are good examples of this type of bias. We must be careful as we call on students to answer questions that we call on a variety of students—and that we look students in the eye when we speak to them. The exception to this rule is for students from Native American and some Asian cultures where looking directly into the eye is an insult.

One of the most unfortunate ways that schools have excluded students of minority races and students with learning differences is to isolate them into special programs. I understand that students with special needs often require the services of professionals trained to help with their needs or handicaps; those are not the students to whom I refer here. I refer, instead, to students who are relegated to compensatory programs because they are poor or belong to a minority group, and so an assumption is made that they must need additional help. When we make those kinds of assumptions, we often get what we expect: Students are not expected to do well, so they don't do well.

Manning and Kovach (2003) say that "over 50% of all minority high school students exhibit deficiencies:

- Only 1% of black 17-year-olds can comprehend information from a specialized text, such as the science section of a daily newspaper. This compares with just over 8% of white youth of the same age.
- Only 20% of black high school students can comprehend a less specialized text that over 50% of whites understand.
- In elementary algebra, which is considered a gateway course for college preparation, only 1% of black students can successfully solve a problem involving more than one basic step in its solution; 10% of white students can solve such a problem.
- Although 70% of white high school students have mastered computation with fractions, only 3% of black students have done so.
- By the time they graduate from high school, black and Latino students are reading on the same level as white eighth graders." (p. 28)

Often what these students actually need is individual help, not special programs. Response to intervention (RTI) is an effort through ESEA legislation to do just that. Through RTI programs, students who are struggling are given individual or small group help before they fail.

Many of us learned in our college classes about the controversy over nature versus nurture. Are we born with a fixed intelligence? Which is more important, our genes or our environment? Current brain research indicates that it is not nature *versus* nurture but rather nature *and* nurture. We are all born into this world hardwired to learn and to learn at a very high level. If you don't believe me watch a two-year-old for a while: Children at that age are constantly exploring, tasting, smelling, watching, listening to, and verbalizing with the world that they are trying to grasp.

Why then do some students come to school without the necessary prerequisites for success? That is where nurture comes in to play. Learning should be encouraged from a very young age—but because of consequences and stresses placed on many home environments, parents are too exhausted, too stressed, or too ill to provide the nurturance that is needed. Add to that the fact that many children today go to day care from the time they are old enough to leave the house. While many day care facilities are excellent and provide wonderful reinforcement for children, many are understaffed and undertrained to provide the kind of nurturing needed for maximum development. Children from poverty rarely get the high quality preschool programs that are expensive and often only available to their more affluent peers. Without national standards and regulations for preschool programs parents and caregivers are often left with nothing more than a babysitting program for their children. This only widens the gap further for children entering kindergarten and first grade without the prerequisite skills expected at that age. Schools that do not have safeguards in place to understand the reasons for the gaps may mistakenly believe that the gaps are neurological rather than from lack of vocabulary or the enriched experiences of the other children in the classroom who have been exposed to books, vocabulary, and numbers early.

Students once thought to have learning problems may simply need encouragement to succeed and the individual tutoring to help them catch up with their peers. They also need teachers who have been empowered by being trained on how to modify for culture and poverty.

UNREALITY

The fourth type of bias is unreality or the misinformation about a group, event, or contribution. One of the most famous studies in education points up this type of bias. Teachers were given new students, all of average intelligence. Some teachers were told that their students were above average in intelligence; some were told their students were below average. At the end of the experiment, it was found that students who were expected to do very well did very well and students who were expected to do poorly did poorly.

In the teachers' lounge, in the hallway, and in faculty meetings, other teachers may share with you their opinions of students in your classroom. Smile and thank them but lean on hard data and the demonstration of understanding that you see in your classroom. Let your students know that you believe in them and that you expect their best.

One school year, the teachers in my school started the year by telling students that this school year was a whole new ballgame. It did not matter what they had done in our classrooms last year or what their brother or sister had done. Beginning that year, we expected them to do their best work and we were not going to accept anything less than excellent work. As a matter of fact, we gave work back to them if it was not done well and provided additional help for them outside of the regular class time to redo their work. As a result, the quality of student work went up, and scores on state and national exams went up as well.

Ask yourself, "What are my expectations for my students?" Make sure that you have high expectations for all students, not just the pretty ones, not just those from the same ethnic group as you, and certainly not just those the group in the teachers' lounge told you would make it.

As educators, here are some things that we can do to make a difference:

- We must place highly qualified and experienced teachers in education programs where there are high poverty rates. There are great first year teachers, but

Education Trust says that teachers with as much as three years experience make as much difference in the classroom as if we had removed 10 of the students.

- We must enable teachers and other educators through quality professional development in elements of effective pedagogy that apply to culturally diverse classrooms.
- We need to find teachers who believe in their heart of hearts that all children can learn and that they are capable of teaching all children.
- We need a "no excuses" policy that lets students know we will never give up on them.
- We must find ways to both let our students know we see the potential they possess and to mirror it back to them. This is especially important to children "who have been labeled or oppressed, in understanding their personal power to reframe their life narratives from damaged victim or school failure to resilient survivor and successful learner" (Benard, 2003, p. 120).

SELECTIVITY

The fifth bias is selectivity or the single interpretation of an issue, situation, or conditions. Help your students to see things from more than one perspective and to find more than one way to solve a problem. According to Payne (2001), students from poverty often laugh when disciplined. This comes from survival on the streets, where to show fear could literally cost them their lives. The role of the teacher is not to show intolerance for this reaction but to help the student to know that, although that reaction may be appropriate on the street, in the larger world, to laugh at your boss when reprimanded would probably cost you your job. Students may need to be taught the proper way to respond in the world beyond the streets. This is one of the ways that we build resiliency in our students. According to Benard (2003) resiliency is the ability to achieve success in spite of circumstances. When working with students from poverty, building resiliency should be a major goal.

In addition, we must be open to differing opinions and differing perspectives. Helping students to look at situations from varying points of view will help them to be better problem solvers. Often, understanding the underlying problem is half the journey to finding the solution. We find the underlying problem when we understand different perspectives. In a global world, it is important to be able to listen to others and to see their viewpoint even when we do not agree with that viewpoint.

ISOLATION

The sixth bias is isolation or the separating of groups. In the classroom it is important to build a camaraderie among the students that fosters communication and acceptance. In a small school experiment in which we actively built teams of students within each classroom (from elementary school through high school) we were surprised to find that students did not really know each other unless they happened to be on an athletic team together or friends outside of class. If that was true of a little school, how much more true it must be in large schools.

It takes a conscious effort to build rapport in a classroom, and it can only be done if students have opportunities to talk with each other and to work together on the learning. Use the cooperative learning model, which requires grouping of students to mimic the makeup of the classroom. In other words, groups should include both male and female students and students from different ethnic groups. Johnson, Johnson, and Holubec (1994) say that students will never sit differently in the lunchroom if they don't sit differently in the classroom. Part of building relationships with students is to create a learning community in the classroom just as you would create a learning community with your colleagues. Remember that learning communities have shared goals and shared problems to solve, and they work with a collegial spirit to attain their goals. This more closely mirrors how most of the world learns outside the northern European model and will help to build those important relationships.

The Road to Closing the Achievement Gap

Despite national imagery full of high-flying concepts like "equal opportunity" and "level playing field," English-learners, low-income, and minority students do not get the extra school support they need to catch up to their more advantaged peers; they all too frequently receive less than do other students.

— Carmen G. Arroyo

For years we have been trying to close the gaps in achievement, particularly for students from diverse cultures and poverty. If we consider the enormous resources including financial and human energy put into this effort, we are still disappointed with the results thus far. As stated in Chapter 2, the gap has even widened in some segments. Zeichner (2003), along with

Williams (2003), suggest that there are some factors that must be examined and dealt with if we are to close the gaps forever.

THE URBAN ACHIEVEMENT GAP: FACT VERSUS FICTION

According to Williams (2003), the prevailing attitude in many circles is that there is an achievement gap because that is all we can expect from urban students. Add to this the fact that so many of these students are sent to special education at an early age—often not because of cognition problems but because they learn differently—and we have a recipe for disaster. As discussed earlier, studies by Education Trust (Arroyo, 2008) show that high poverty areas tend to have teachers with less experience, less pay, and a high turnover rate. This is for students who, perhaps more than any other students, need stability in their lives and teachers who are firm and consistent and who want to be in their school and classroom every day.

The solutions are not confined to the schools but must be a part of a unified effort on the part of national, state, and local entities that work hand in hand with parents and the schools. In order for poor students to be able to compete on a level playing field, they must have the quality health, nutrition, and other resources that are a part of the package of essentials provided to children who do not come from poverty. Wang and Kovach (1996) agree: "Narrowly conceived plans and commitment that focus only on schools will not solve the growing problems that must be addressed to ensure success of the many children and youth who have not fared well under the current system of service delivery" (p. 19).

Payne (2001) says that wealth is measured in the amount of available resources—not just money. Resources include such things as strong support systems, role models, ability to work within the middle-class framework (which is the basis for most schools), physical and mental health, and money to purchase both goods and services. For those in poverty the same resources are not as readily available as for those in more affluent surroundings. Until there is dialogue and cooperation among the political and social entities that can help to provide these resources, what can be done in schools is limited. It is limited, but it is very significant.

WHAT CAN TEACHERS DO?

While we have limited control over the decisions of political entities (for example, we can vote for those who understand the problem and are willing to do something about it), we have direct control over what happens to the urban poor in regard to education in our classrooms.

Examine Our Beliefs

First, as teachers we must assess our own belief systems about students. What preconceived ideas do we bring to the classroom? What are our expectations for our students? Do we bring biases to the classroom, and, if so, are we willing to rethink our biases based on what we have learned? Do we truly believe that all kids can learn and learn at a high level? We must have honest dialogue about our own culture and how that is different from the culture of our students. In your learning community groups you might ask questions such as "In my school what difference does color or race make?" "What about ethnicity?" "Does language background make a difference in the classroom?"

Do Not Tolerate Bias

Second, we must be determined that we will not tolerate belittling or demonstrations of bias in our classrooms and that we will be consistent about enforcing that idea.

Help Students Know Each Other

Third, we need to incorporate ideas for helping our students get to know each other and to be able to dialogue with each other in nonaggressive formats. Use icebreakers at the beginning of school such as the Find Someone Who tool in Form 4.1. In the

Form 4.1 Find Someone Who . . .

Directions

- Give students a list of questions.
- Have students find other students in the room who can answer one of the questions.
- Instruct students to initial or write their first name by their answers.
- Require students to get a different signature on each question.

Find Someone Who . . .

Directions: Ask a different person to sign for each of the following.

Find someone who . . .

Likes the same sport as you

Has a blue car

Has two brothers

Plans to go to college in another state

Had an unusual summer job

Plans to become a lawyer

Likes to work with computers

Has a birthday in December

Has been to Disney World

Has an unusual hobby

Variation

Directions: Use this tool as a review after material has been studied. Instead of personal questions, use questions about the lesson. For example

Find Someone Who . . .

Can define *denominator*

Find Someone Who tool, students locate a different person for each of the questions listed. The first person to complete his or her list might get an extrinsic reward or special recognition. Sometimes teachers vary this with a bingo-type format where students "win" when they get their paper signed either across or diagonally.

Build Resiliency

Fifth, according to Bonnie Benard (2003), resilience is the ability to achieve in spite of negative circumstances. Following are some things that we can do to help build resiliency in our students:

- Directly teach students cause and effect—things do not generally happen because of "luck" or forces beyond our control but are influenced by our decisions.
- Directly teach decision making, self-control, and assertiveness.
- Model appropriate social behavior in school and the workplace.
- Help to instill an attitude of self-worth and self-efficacy. Marzano (2001) says that self-efficacy is the gatekeeper to motivation in children from poverty. Self-efficacy is different from self-esteem. Self-esteem means, "I feel good about myself and I think I can be successful." While this is important, it is often built on "I think and I feel" rather than on fact. Self-efficacy is built on past experience and it says, "This is hard but I have been successful before and I know I can be successful again." Use multiple intelligences to help students identify their strengths (we are all gifted in at least three of these intelligences) and show them how to build up their weaknesses.
- Help to move students toward a positive outlook for the future.

Promote Close Bonds

Get to know your students as individuals rather than as a sea of faces that you encounter each day. Talk to them, give them individual attention, provide opportunities for discussion, and let them know that we are learners together. One of the most important things that a good teacher does is to promote self-confidence in students and to guide them to becoming self-directed learners. Think of your classroom as a community of learners with yourself included. We know from the research on culture that for students from outside the northern European culture of the typical classroom, relationship must come before substance. In the dominant culture of the classroom, teachers provide substance first and create relationships along the way. For most other cultures a relationship must be established before the curriculum is taught.

Provide opportunities for your students to get to know one another and to know you as their mentor, coach, instructor, and guide. Insist that students respect one another and you. First, be a model for this by showing respect for them, and then be certain that bullying, name calling, ethnic jokes or remarks, put downs, and disrespect are not tolerated in your classroom. Discuss with your class why you are doing this and be consistent. Don't let someone get away with negative or harmful behavior one day and enforce the rule on another day. Consistency is essential if real change is to come about. Steven Covey (1989) calls it the 28 day rule: If we practice a behavior for 28 days, it becomes internalized.

Value and Encourage Education

You will find that the value of education varies among your students and that much of what has influenced them has come before they entered your class. Payne (2001) says that all three socioeconomic groups—poor, middle class, and upper class—value education but in different ways. The poor value it but as an abstract entity. After all, when you are constantly trying to feed your family and keep the bill collectors away, education is not your primary concern. When working with students and parents from poverty, it is important to point out that education keeps them from being cheated and gives them opportunities to solve economic problems. This is usually more productive than telling them that it is important to do well in school so they can go to the college of their choice.

Kids from poverty tend to live in the here and now. What will education do for them right now?

Students from the middle class value education because it is a means to a better paying job and a good school. Students from the upper class view education as another rung in the networking ladder; for them, it is important to go to the right schools and to meet the right people who can help influence their future.

Understanding these differences in attitudes will give you a starting place for working with students and their parents to help them understand the importance of learning. For example, when people know how to use math effectively, they are less likely to be cheated, they are able to plan for the future so they can be independent, they have more opportunities to advance, and they are more likely to have the lives they desire. Telling students that they need to learn so that they can go to the next grade or pass a test really does not do much for building long-term intrinsic motivation.

In addition, the brain learns more effectively those things that have meaning to the individual. According to Jensen (1997), the gatekeeper to the brain is *meaning*: If the material has no meaning to the student, it is not likely to be remembered. The bottom line is to tell students up front why the lesson is important.

Other Guidelines

Other things we can do to build resiliency include

- Using a high-warmth/low-criticism style of interaction
- Setting and enforcing clear boundaries such as rules, norms, and laws
- Encouraging supportive relationships with many caring others
- Promoting the sharing of responsibilities, service to others, "required helpfulness"
- Providing access to resources for the basic needs of housing, employment, health care, and recreation
- Expressing high, realistic expectations for success
- Encouraging goal setting and mastery

- Encouraging prosocial development of values and life skills, such as cooperation
- Providing leadership, decision making, and other opportunities for meaningful participation
- Appreciating the unique talents of each individual

Promote Diversity

The fifth thing teachers can do is provide accurate information about cultural groups through straightforward discussions of race, ethnicity, and other cultural differences. This information should come from a wide variety of resources, not just the text or one resource. Be sure your information includes both cross-cultural similarities and cross-cultural differences: There are probably just as many differences within a culture as there are between cultures.

McCune, Stephens, and Lowe (1999) recommend that teachers keep the following ideas in mind as they promote diversity:

- Remember that cultural diversity in our schools and society can be recognized and appreciated without denunciation of Western values and cultural traditions.
- Recognize that there are as many differences within a group as there are between groups.
- Remember that there is a positive correlation between teacher expectations and academic performance.
- Remember to hold high expectations for students, regardless of ethnicity, gender, or exceptionality.
- Remember that self-esteem and academic achievement go hand in hand.
- Remember that there is no single approach to meeting the educational needs of all children in a multicultural classroom.
- Remember that multiculturalism is not a "minority thing" and it includes us all.
- Remember that human understanding is a lifelong endeavor.

Which Teaching and Learning Strategies Make the Most Difference in Closing the Gap?

We speak a great deal about using "best practices" but what are they and how do we know that an instructional practice really will make a difference in students' lives? I always say that we need to teach vocabulary first to our students so I will walk the talk here and begin by defining what makes an instructional practice considered best practice.

WHAT IS A BEST PRACTICE?

An instructional strategy is considered to be a best practice when it has been proven through research to have a high effect on student learning. The research that leads to this conclusion has, at a minimum, the following characteristics:

1. It is based on the results of multiple studies. So many times I have heard educators say, "I know this will work for you because it worked for my school." One incidence of success does not make a best-practice strategy.

2. The studies are peer reviewed to make sure that the evidence is based on a number of studies and that it is free from bias on the part of the researchers involved in the studies.

3. We usually have an "effect size" that will tell us how much difference the practice will make when it is used correctly in the classroom. Effect size is a unit of measurement in statistics that "expresses the increase or decrease in achievement of the experimental group (the group of students who are exposed to a specific instructional technique) in standard deviation units" (Marzano, Pickering, & Pollock, 2001, p. 4). Effect sizes can be translated into percentile points, which are more often used by teachers. Conversion tables are available for doing this. In general, Marzano et al. used the work of researcher Jacob Cohen to interpret effect sizes this way: (1) an effect size of .20 or an 8% gain is considered to be small, (2) an effect size of .50 or 19% gain is considered to be medium improvement, and (3) an effect size of .80 or a 29% gain is considered to be a large gain (p. 6).

No Child Left Behind (NCLB) is a reauthorization of Elementary and Secondary Education Act (ESEA) in 2001. The

Individuals with Disabilities Education Act (IDEA) of 2004 is a federal law ensuring services "to improve the academic achievement and functional performance of children with disabilities including the use of scientifically based instructional practices, to the maximum extent possible" (U.S. Department of Education, 2004). Both of these federal legislations call for students to be taught using research-based practices that have been shown to make a difference in student learning, "holding schools, local education agencies, and states accountable for improving the academic achievement of all students . . . [and] promoting schoolwide reform and ensuring the access of all children to effective scientifically-based instructional strategies" (U.S. Department of Education, 2001).

This chapter is devoted to providing information to help teachers of students from poverty and other cultural influences as a guide to help their students reach greater success rates and at the same time provide efficacy for the teacher.

HIGH EXPECTATIONS: WHY THEY MATTER

As stated in Chapter 4, it is important to have high expectations for all students, not just those who exhibit good study skills. There are some obvious reasons as to why this is important. We know, for example, that when we have high expectations for students we are more likely to provide a rich and rigorous curriculum. There are deeper reasons that get at the heart of research on how our brains learn and remember. Students from poverty often have negative experiences with school from an early age when the instructional strategies and the classroom materials do not match their cultures. They may have low self-efficacy in terms of school while enjoying high self-efficacy in other aspects of their lives. Students who experience high self-efficacy in terms of social relationships with their peers and low self-efficacy in terms of learning may choose to act out in the classroom in order to show their strengths in relations with their friends. Marzano et al. (2001)

discuss the importance of reinforcing effort in students and in providing recognition for work well done. They cite a study by Van Overwalle and De Metsenaere (Marzano et al.) in which these researchers found that "students who were taught about the relationship between effort and achievement achieved more than students who were taught techniques for time management and comprehension of new material" (p. 95). Providing students with praise based on effort has a high effect size on student learning—a 27% gain in achievement (Tileston & Darling, 2009, p. 172).

The Role of the Self-System in Learning

It is the self-system that directs our attention either toward the learning or toward daydreaming. The self-system is the "Do I wanna?" part of the learning that takes place at the beginning of a lesson. Students decide very quickly whether they will engage or not. In order to gain students' attention for the learning, we need to understand how this powerful system works and what we can do as teachers to activate the system in positive ways. There are several factors that affect the self-system of the brain. The following factors automatically (without much conscious thought) direct our attention:

- *Self-Attributes.* This factor refers to the way in which the student sees himself or herself. It is not limited to a one-dimensional view but may vary with attributes. For example, a student may see himself one way in regard to athletics, another in regard to personal appearance, and yet another in regard to learning.
- *Self and Others.* This factor refers to the way a student sees herself in regard to groups or units of people. In other words, what is her status in regard to her peers? To her family? To others? Our culture plays an important part in this and is also responsible for our differences.

- *Nature of the World.* This factor refers to the way in which the student sees himself or herself in regard to the world. Is the world friendly or hostile? Marzano (1998) reminds us that students at this stage either perceive that they have control over their lives or they don't. If they perceive that they do not, then they may believe that someone or some force in the world controls the things that happen to them. Students from poverty often believe that they have no locus of control over events in their lives—they often blame "bad luck" for the negatives. We have to directly teach these students that it is effort, not luck, that helps them to be successful in the classroom.

- *Efficacy.* This factor deals with "the extent to which an individual believes she or he has the resources or power to change a situation" (Marzano, 2001, p. 51). This belief is not just based on "I think and I feel," as in the case of self-esteem but on facts derived from previous experiences. For example, if a student has had positive experiences with math in the past, she is more likely to have positive self-efficacy about math now. This is just one of the reasons why it is so important that students experience success in our classrooms. The success must be genuine; however, watering down material does not build self-efficacy.

- *Purpose.* This category of the self-system has to do with the students' perceptions about their lives' purposes. We need to let students know why they are learning the material and how it will help them personally.

Through the factors listed above, the student trying to decide whether to pay attention to the learning or to continue daydreaming will consciously and unconsciously activate the self-system by examining the importance of the assignment, utilizing the degree to which they have positive self-efficacy, and by taking into consideration his or her emotional response to the learning. Let's examine each of these in light of today's learners and what we can do as teachers to help students use this system to help them learn.

Importance

Marzano and Kendall (2008) explain that what an individual considers to be important is probably a function of the extent to which it meets one of two conditions: it is perceived as instrumental in satisfying a basic need, or it is perceived as instrumental in the attainment of a personal goal. Using these two measures, here are some ways that the classroom teacher can enhance the students' beliefs about the importance of the learning.

- Tell students up front why the learning is important. Explain how they might use it in the real world. Begin by asking students to tell you why it is important to them (you will need to guide them at first). Marzano and Kendall suggest that we use "short or extended written and oral constructed-response formats" (p. 164).
- Prior to the learning, build a connection between what the students are about to learn and what they already know.

The brain seeks connections, and where there are none, chaos can follow. *What Every Teacher Should Know About Effective Teaching Strategies* (Tileston, 2004a) provides numerous examples of how to make connections effectively. One of the teaching practices that seems highly effective in helping students make connections between previous and new learning is to begin by asking students to create a nonlinguistic organizer about the prior learning. This can be done in small groups or individually. A nonlinguistic organizer is a graphic picture of the learning that relies on structure rather than words. A mind map is an example of a nonlinguistic organizer. Chapter 4 provides an example of a mind map for science class.

What if I am introducing a unit of study for which my students have no prior knowledge? In that case, I must create the connection. Whistler and Williams (1990) use the example of introducing at the elementary level the book *Henry Huggins* by Beverly Cleary. In this book, the main character finds a dog and brings it home only to have the owner show up and want his dog back. To build empathy—one of the skills necessary for understanding—a teacher might begin the lesson by asking students to tell what they would do in a similar situation. Whistler and Williams call this strategy "We'd rather," and it places students into similar situations as the main characters to see what they would do. Teachers give children choices, such as to hide the dog, to give the dog back willingly, to pretend that you don't have the dog, or to work out an arrangement with the owner so that you can see the dog.

We can also make the learning personally important to our students by asking them to write personal goals for the learning. As teachers, we model this activity by making a visual model of our declarative and procedural goals—what we want the students to know and what we want the students to be able to do as a result of the learning—for the unit or lesson. We should take the time to go over those goals with the students and then have them make two or three personal goals based on this information. By doing this, we not only provide a personal connection to the learning, but we provide a way for students to examine how well they are doing in their own work. Come back to these goals often and show students how to modify their personal goals when things are not working. Forms 5.1 and 5.2 are elementary and secondary examples of how this might look.

Efficacy

The exercises in Forms 5.1 and 5.2 also help to build efficacy in our students. By providing a way for students to self-evaluate their own learning, we provide a basis for them to monitor and adjust their work to succeed. We also

Form 5.1 Elementary Example of Goal Setting

For the book *Bubba the Cowboy Prince: A Fractured Texas Tale* by Helen Ketteman, I have provided some learning goals. The declarative goals are that you will know

- The sequence of events
- The importance of the sequence of events to the story
- The main characters and how they contribute to the story
- The main idea of the story

The procedural goals are that you will be able to

- Compare and contrast Bubba with other versions of Cinderella
- Identify how the author uses humor
- Compare ways that the author uses setting, main characters, theme, and activities in unique ways as compared to the more traditional Cinderella
- Write your own version of Cinderella

What are some personal goals that you have made for yourself?

- I want to be able to identify how setting, characters, and theme are used in a variety of Cinderella stories so that I can make a decision about my writing.
- I want to create a humorous version of Cinderella that uses a funny animal instead of a person.
- I want to learn to use humor like the author of Bubba does.

Form 5.2 Secondary Example of Goal Setting

John Hersey wrote a book about the horrors of Hiroshima from the viewpoint of an observer who is not politically connected to either side in the war. While this is difficult to do, he did a great job of presenting the facts and allowing the reader to make up her own mind about the politics, ethics, and emotional reaction.

For your lesson on John Hersey and his account of Hiroshima, I have set the following objectives.

The declarative objectives are that you will know

- The definitions of the vocabulary associated with this lesson
- The responsibilities associated with impartial reporting
- The key attributes used by Hersey to report his accounts as an observer

The procedural objectives are that you will be able to

- Infer information through generalizing, predicting, summarizing, and hypothesizing
- Analyze given information
- Create your own written product through synthesizing, organizing, planning, and problem solving

What are some personal goals that you have for the learning?

- I want to understand how to write impartially, even when everything around you is going wrong.
- I want to know when it is appropriate to write in an impartial way and when it is not.
- I want to be able to tell the difference between facts and opinions.
- I want the opportunity to write something from an observer's point of view. I don't know if I can do that.

build self-efficacy by ensuring that students have positive experiences with the learning. One of the best ways of doing that is to provide consistent and constructive feedback often. Do not rely on blanket statements, such as "good going," to make a difference in self-efficacy. The work of Marzano (2001) shows that when feedback is consistent and when it is specific, the effect on student learning is huge. Without this process, the results may be disastrous. We may even be helping students to move backward in regard to success when we rely only on blanket statements or when we give praise that is not deserved.

Learned helplessness is a condition that develops over time when the person experiences failure after failure. This is a condition with which we deal when students come to us from poverty, from the negative effects of the urban city, and with only negative experiences with learning. It is important to note that learned helplessness is just that—it is learned by one's environment. Altering the perception and experiences of the learning can change it.

Emotional Response

Enough cannot be said about the importance of emotion on learning. Emotion has the power to shut down or to enhance quality learning. While it is important how each student feels about the learning, about the instructor, about the classroom, and about himself or herself in the learning situation, these feelings are critical to the urban learner. Inner-city poor will pay little attention in a classroom where they feel a threat—emotional, physical, social, or mental. The relationship with the teacher is paramount in reaching these students. This does not mean that the teacher must be their buddy, but rather that the teacher must exhibit understanding and warmth toward all of the students. Such a teacher seeks to understand the special problems of the urban learner, seeks to make connections for learners with various resources to enhance the students' lives, and to teach in a variety of ways so that all students are reached.

WE HAVE THEIR ATTENTION—NOW WHAT?

Once students begin a task or decide to pay attention, the metacognitive system of the brain takes over. This system relies heavily on goals that have been set by the student (either consciously or unconsciously) and on whether the student will follow through when things are not going according to plan. Directly teach students how to set personal goals for the learning. Once the goals have been set, visit them often and ask students if they are meeting their personal goals. If not, ask why not and what can you do to assist them. Teachers can model goal setting by sharing with students instructional goals for the learning. Form 5.3 is an example of how that might look.

Since the metacognitive system is going to set goals with or without our input, it is to our advantage as teachers to promote quality goals by explicitly demonstrating how we set objectives for the learning and by asking our students to make personal goals. We can enhance the work of the metacognitive system in our students by doing the following:

1. Set goals for the learning and share those goals (in writing or in pictures for young learners) with students.

2. Explicitly show students how to set personal goals for the learning. Form 5.4, I have given you an example of a graphic organizer to help students create their own goals for the learning.

3. Provide linguistic and nonlinguistic organizers as a guide to help students set goals. The example provided in Form 5.4 is a linguistic organizer since it relies on words to convey the objective. An example of a nonlinguistic organizer would be a mind map in which students rely on pictures and only a few words to show their goals.

4. Demonstrate to students how we use positive self-talk as we work through problems. Tell students what you do when you encounter a word you do not know; what do you do

Form 5.3 Personal Goals for the Learning

In this unit we will learn

1. How to identify geometric shapes

2. The characteristics of geometric shapes

3. Where we find geometric shapes in the real world

What is something you would like to know about shapes?

How will you meet your goal?

Did you meet your goal? If so, how? If not, why not?

Form 5.4   Teacher Goals for the Learning

Title of Unit: Why Matter Matters

Part One: The States of Matter

Standard 5. Understands the structure and properties of matter

5.1 Knows that matter has different states (such as liquid, solid, gas) and that each state has distinct physical properties; some common materials such as water can be changed from one state to another by heating and cooling.

5.9 Knows that states of matter depend on molecular arrangement and motion.

Part Two: The Properties of Matter

5.3 Knows that substances can be classified by their physical and chemical properties (e.g., magnetism, conductivity, density, solubility, boiling and melting points)

5.4 Knows that many elements can be grouped according to similar properties (e.g., highly reactive metals, less-reactive metals, highly reactive nonmetals, almost completely nonreactive gases)

Standards were taken from the Mid-Continent Regional Education Laboratory list of benchmarks for science from http://www.mcrel.org/compendium/standar Details.asp?=2&standardID=8 on 8/4/09.

when you are working through a math problem and you cannot get the correct answer? What about a science experiment that goes badly? This is especially important when personal goals are not going well and we must work through or revamp our plans to carry out the goals. One of the major complaints about all students—and about urban learners in particular—is that they exhibit impulsivity both in behavior and in learning. We control impulsivity by having a plan and by knowing what to do when the plan is not working. This ability must be taught to our students; they will not come to our classrooms with that knowledge. We can only know that the plans are not working if we walk around the room often to see and hear what students are doing and by providing very specific feedback.

5. Provide students with a rubric or matrix prior to the learning so that they know the expectations and so that they know what we mean by quality work. I am convinced that more students would work at a quality level if they know what that was. In *What Every Teacher Should Know About Student Assessment* (Tileston, 2004b), I talk about how to create rubrics and matrices for student work. We should never take a grade for a product, from homework to projects, without first giving students a matrix or rubric that specifically gives them the expectations. To do otherwise is a "gotcha" and it is not fair. By providing a rubric or matrix up front, we take the personality out of the grading. The rubric states explicitly the expectation and the point value. If the student does the work, the student gets the grade; my personal feelings toward the student, her past work, or his behavior do not matter. This is one of the best ways that I know to begin to level the playing field for all students. In Form 5.5 have provided a graphic organizer for you to build your own rubric with the specific attributes that make something of quality. Form 5.5 begins with an example of one of the components of a persuasive essay and the parts that will make it quality. By specifically providing this information to students we do two things: (1) ensure that students know specifically what is expected and (2) make the grading consistent and fair. The elements are either there or they are not.

Form 5.5 Matrix

Components	Point Value	Specific Attributes
Opening paragraph	15%	1. Clearly states purpose 2. Provides the author's perspective 3. Draws the reader to know more
Each major part of the essay follows with point values for each part and the attributes that contribute to the quality.		

GENERAL IDEAS FOR COGNITION

I have discussed the importance of giving instructional strategies that affect the self- and metacognitive systems of the brain. Scaffolding is one of the important ways that we help students understand the learning at a deeper level.

Provide scaffolding to bridge the gap between how students learn in the home-neighborhood environment and how they learn in school. Zeichner (2003) says there are two ways that we can build this scaffolding. One is by incorporating the students' culture and language into the classroom. The other is by explicitly teaching students about the culture of the classroom, which is built, in part, on the middle-class structures. Let's look at what this means in terms of classroom instruction and the environment.

Incorporating the Language and Culture

Before we can incorporate the languages and cultures of our students into our classroom, we must make ourselves aware of what they are. We need to have an understanding of the neighborhoods from which our students come, as well.

Next, we must use the resources that our students bring with them to enhance the learning. For example, storytelling is a part of many cultures and, in particular, of Mexican American, African American, and Native American households. Teachers who can put learning into the context of a story are helping these students to learn in a modality that is comfortable and familiar to them. Daniel Pink (2007) says that in a global world the ability to talk to people using stories is an important 21st century skill. Most of the world learns through stories.

Another way that we can enhance the learning of our students is to use examples from their worlds. Provide writing opportunities that incorporate the experiences and the cultures from which they come. Provide examples that incorporate those things with which they are familiar. I talk about Kay Toliver in many of my books. Kay Toliver taught math in an inner-city school with some tremendous results. When she taught fractions to her students, she didn't say, "You need to know this so that you can be successful." Instead, she told them specifically how learning fractions would help them to be successful. For example, knowing fractional parts will keep them from being cheated when they buy food by the slice, such as pizza. There is a big difference between 1/16 of a pizza for $1.00 and 1/4 of a pizza for the same amount of money. Students from the urban areas tend to live in the present: they want to know how the learning will help them now. We also scaffold when we provide structure that is often not part of their lives outside of school. Scaffolding should be used, rather than watering down curriculum, because students have gaps in learning and experience. For example, in math class a group of students are struggling with understanding the differences in decimals and fractions. Past educational programs might assume that there is a cognitive problem that would best be addressed in special education or other remedial programs. However, now we know that students from poverty may not have the vocabulary to understand the concepts. For example, if I do not know the terms *denominator* or *numerator* or even the word *decimal*, I will have great difficulty learning this objective.

By scaffolding the learning, a teacher would first make sure that every student understands the vocabulary of the unit and then the teacher might use a graphic organizer, such as the one in Form 5.6, to help students understand the concept. By doing this, the teacher has not watered down the content but has taught it using high-level organizers (compare and contrast is a high-level skill).

Students from the inner city often use a form of language referred to by Payne (2001) as *casual register*, which basically is the language of the street. It is unrealistic to believe that students will come to us knowing the more formal register of the classroom. Payne even suggests that for these students we might allow them to first write in the casual register and lead them to rewrite in the more formal register of the classroom and professional writing.

Teachers who know their students and their cultures will understand that students who do not speak English well, i.e., English language learners, may be embarrassed to speak or read aloud in English in the classroom. They often can speak more words than we think because they exhibit shyness in the classroom when asked to speak. Use patience with these students as they become comfortable with their surroundings.

Also know that English language learners often lack the language acquisition skills to process and embed English words into the long-term memory systems of the brain. This is especially true of factual information such as dates, vocabulary, and lists, which are stored in the semantic pathway of the brain. The semantic pathway needs a connector so that we can retrieve the information that is stored. We can help them to put information into long-term memory by relying on context and visuals to help with the learning. Again, nonlinguistic organizers are a good way to help these students process information in the classroom. When learning vocabulary, I have used a visual organizer, using pictures with the words, to help my students learn the terms. Form 5.7 is an example of a visual organizer for learning vocabulary when the primary language is not English.

Compare two things.

Living		Nonliving
	Three ways in which they are alike 1. They take up space 2. They have weight 3. They have a variety of sizes and shapes	

Contrast two things.

Living		Nonliving
	How they are different? 1. Movement 2. Respiration 3. Needs	

Form 5.7 Using Pictures and Symbols to Learn Vocabulary

Vocabulary Word	Definition	Words, Symbols, Pictures to Help Me Remember
Creating	Generating new products	
Analysis	Breaking whole into parts	
Problem solving	Clarify problem, generate solutions, test hypothesis, evaluate	Clarify Generate Test Evaluate
Inference	Generalizing, predicting, summarizing	If . . . , then. . . .

Since the semantic memory system of the brain is the system that stores facts, vocabulary, places, and names, we can help English language learners by giving the words symbols or connectors to help the students store the information in a more appropriate context.

Explicitly Teaching the Culture of the Classroom

We cannot assume that students who come to us from poverty and from other cultures will automatically know and understand what Payne (2001) calls the *hidden* rules of the dominant classroom culture. For the most part, these hidden rules are based on middle-class ideals and values and on schools that were set up using a northern European model.

For example, we often tell students that they need to learn given material because it will help them get into the college of their choice or because it will make them more successful later on in life. While that is important for all students to know and believe, we must work with our students in terms of what is important to them. For many urban learners survival is paramount, and they want to know how learning is going to help them now. How will it enhance their status with their friends? How will it help them to survive? How will it keep them from being cheated? Begin here and then tell them that it will also provide opportunities for them in the future because you believe in them and that they are capable of great things.

Help students to understand that there is a set of behaviors and communication standards that work on the street and there is another set of behaviors and speech patterns that will make them successful in school and at work. Lindsey, Robbins, and Terrell (2009) remind us, "School systems must recognize that marginalized populations have to be at least bicultural and that this status creates a distinct set of issues to which the system must be equipped to respond" (p. 99). Payne (2001) uses the example of a student who laughs when disciplined. The rule of the street is that you do not show fear—it could get you killed. However, when disciplined at school or when a boss talks to you about an error, to laugh is to show disrespect. We cannot assume that our students will know that information without explicitly being told the difference in what is acceptable on the street and what is acceptable in the classroom. This information is important for our students to know, and it should be delivered in a voice that is polite, friendly, and nonjudgmental—not in an authoritative or superior voice.

When students misbehave, they need to know the other choices that they have and how to plan so that they are not impulsive in their behaviors. The language of some cultures is physical and loud. These students may not have the resources to know how to react otherwise. In cases such as those, we must explicitly teach them the difference. Cooperative learning programs are a great way to teach some of these skills. Students from poverty tend to be visual and kinesthetic learners; they like movement and they like working with their friends. As a matter of fact, students from cultures such as Native American believe strongly in sharing—materials and information; it is part of their culture. We can help to incorporate the cultural beliefs into the classroom by providing ways for students to share some of the materials and by using cooperative learning. Students need structure, however, or they will be a discipline nightmare. Just putting students into groups is not cooperative learning. Cooperative learning is very structured and incorporates social and emotional intelligence structures alongside the cognitive structures.

SOME ADDITIONAL THOUGHTS

Based on the work of Williams (2003) and Zeichner (2003) here are some additional guidelines for working with students from poverty.

As teachers, we must

- Truly believe and communicate to our students that all kids can learn—and that they are capable of quality learning, not just superficially covering the material
- Provide a rich, high-level curriculum that gives all students equal opportunities in life NCLB and ESEA demand that we use a research-based curriculum and that all students, regardless of their economic status, have access to a quality curriculum
- Help students to create meaning from the content through a variety of teaching techniques that take into consideration students' backgrounds. Children from poverty and other cultures do not need different instructional practices; they need research-based instructional practices that are modified for culture and poverty

- Provide meaningful learning tasks for all students. No child deserves an inferior education
- Provide the scaffolding necessary for all students to be successful. Scaffolding is different from watering down because it just provides additional structure rather than less rigorous curriculum
- Help students to take pride in their heritages while also teaching them the hidden rules of society
- Create a personal bond with each student and lead students to know that we believe they can learn at a high level
- Provide a variety of resources in the classroom that take into account the cultures of our students

How Do We Deal With Language Acquisition Skills?

English language learners, sometimes called second language learners, comprise a large and growing group of students in this country. By 2024, Hispanic children will comprise the largest group of students in U.S. public schools. As the faces of learners change, so does the role of the school in meeting the challenges of a diverse population that may not speak the English of the classroom. These learners usually fall into one or more of the following groups:

1. Students who have come to this country speaking one or more languages that do not include English. These students may speak little or no English, and English is usually not spoken at home.

2. Students who have come to this country as refugees from other countries. For these students, language may not be the only hurdle they must jump. These students, called limited formal school (LFS) students, may not have had much if any formal education due to the conditions in the countries from which they come.

According to Teachers of English to Speakers of Other Languages (TESOL) of 2001, these students often exhibit the following characteristics:

○ Pre- or semiliterate in their native language
○ Minimal understanding of the function of literacy
○ Performance significantly below grade level
○ A lack of awareness of the school organization and culture

3. Students who speak the informal language of the streets and who do not speak the more formal register related to school and the workplace. Ebonics is an example of this.

The first step for the teacher is to identify the stage of language acquisition in which these students fall. TESOL provides three stages of language learning and the expectations for each of the stages. These stages are fluid; a student may be one stage in a certain setting and another stage in a different setting. For the classroom teacher, identify the stage or stages that are representative of your students.

Beginning Stage

At this stage, students have little or no understanding of the English language. Most of their communication is nonverbal. As they begin to grasp some words these students may initiate questions or statements by using a single word or simple phrases.

These students construct meaning through nonprint visuals such as graphs or other nonlinguistic examples. Although they may construct meaning from some words, the construction of understanding is incomplete.

Intermediate Stage

At the intermediate stage, students have a small vocabulary of essential words and phrases that cover their daily activities. They understand more than they are able to speak although they still require a great deal of repetition from the speaker. At this stage they are using language spontaneously but in a limited way. For example, they may know the basic words to express themselves but lack the terms to make their wishes or thoughts more finite. Their speech is simple and may contain grammatical errors. While they are able to construct more knowledge from texts than at the beginning level, there is still a need for nonlinguistic examples to assist in the understanding.

Advanced Stage

At the advanced stage, students are able to communicate in daily activities. There will still be the occasional structural and lexical errors of the other stages. They can use English in new settings but complex or abstract structures are still difficult. At this level the student should be able to read with fluency and to locate facts within text. They may, however, have difficulty with texts that do not present information in context. Occasional comprehension problems may persist.

General Guidelines for Teachers

The following guidelines are offered to assist the classroom teacher when working with students who do not speak the English language register.

• Students who are learning English move through various developmental stages. The rate at which a student moves is based on the student's background and comprehension of their first language, the degree to which they have been exposed to a formal educational setting, their learning styles, and motivation. According to English for Speakers of Other Languages (ESOL), it may take a language learner as long as five to seven years to acquire English language skills comparable to native English speakers.

- Students will learn language at a quality level when they are given the opportunity to use language in interaction and in meaningful activities. We help to give meaning to the new learning by building on the culture and learning style of the student. Without meaning, there is little motivation to learn. We need to provide personal meaning to all students and in particular English language learners. Most students who are learning a new language learn more efficiently when they can learn in context. For example, a class is beginning a new unit in reading in which they will read a story about Johnny Appleseed. For this unit the teacher begins with a discussion of apples. She asks students to share what they know about apples by providing opportunities for them to discuss how they know about apples from experiences they have had. She is giving apples a context—personal experience.

- Provide many opportunities in the classroom for interaction among the students. By doing this, the teacher is helping students not only acquire the English language acquisition needed for cognitive development, but for social development as well.

- Give feedback often. Language learners need to have goals, and they need to know if they are meeting those goals.

- As the students progress in their use of language, add more challenging activities. Remember that the problem is not intelligence but language acquisition.

- As we look at reading, listening, writing, and speaking, remember that students may be in different stages within these four components of language. For example, a student may be in the beginning stage of writing, an advanced stage of listening, and an intermediate stage of reading at the same time. Learning a language encompasses all four components, and students do not learn them in a linear fashion. For example, students do not learn to speak first then write second. Students move back and forth through reading, listening, writing, and speaking as they acquire language skills.

Working With Diversity

A Teacher's Checklist

Our understanding of the cultures of the classroom has grown substantially in the last 50 years. Yet there is no question that we still struggle with some demographic groups that are outside the dominant culture of the classroom. Lindsey, Robbins, and Terrell (2009) provide three barriers to making effective changes in schools today. They include

1. *The presumption of entitlement,* the belief that the accomplishments of the dominant society are due to the merit and personal qualities of the dominant culture without realizing that other cultures may have had more hurdles to jump to get to the same place.

2. *Systems of oppression and privilege,* "the societal forces that affect individuals due to their membership in a distinct cultural group. Systems of oppression do not require intentional acts by perpetrators; they can be the function of systemic policies and practices" (p. 5).

3. *Unawareness of the need to adapt,* often members of the dominant culture are not aware of the changes that need to occur so that the system is more culturally friendly. They may even believe that *others* need to change, not them.

Form 6.1 is a good visual model to help you as you reflect on this book and to lead the organization to change. Make a checkmark by the things that you have accomplished in regard to diversity. Since learning about diversity takes time, you may want to check those things that are true today and go back periodically to see your growth.

Look for opportunities for networks with other teachers in your building and in other schools to support and encourage yourself.

Stalin supposedly said that he did not need armies to take over countries. He said to give him the country's children for one generation and he would have the country. Who has greater influence over society than teachers? Our influence has the power to change a new generation—for the better and to build a strong middle class.

Form 6.1   Checklist for Your School

The following checklist is offered as a guide for schools as they begin to look for ways to not only narrow the achievement gap but to close it.

What will you do?

In My Country and in My State, I Will

❑ Be cognizant of the attitudes and plans of lawmakers and political candidates in regard to poverty and cultural differences

❑ Be an informed voter

❑ Work for an alignment of federal and state resources to help the poor and to level the educational playing field through better preschool programs

❑ Be proactive in assuring that federal and state measures for success, such as testing, is free of bias or restrictions that single out any particular group

❑ Make sure national standards take into account all students and provide the resources for success—not just to the more affluent areas but also for all students and all teachers

❑ Volunteer to serve on boards and committees, especially those that are setting policies for testing and for resources

In the Community, I Will

❑ Become proactive to provide better health, mental, mentoring, physical, and fiscal resources for my students

❑ Work with parents and other caregivers for solutions

❑ Actively involve parents and members of the community in advisory groups

❑ Set meetings at times that working parents can attend

❑ Provide interpreters for parents who do not speak English

❑ Take into consideration that some parents have come from countries where those in authority have not been fair or friendly. They may be wary of school personnel, especially if they are not citizens

- ❏ Provide opportunities for my students to become proactive in their own communities with projects that include such activities as art, music, writing, starting a newsletter, or providing help at clinics or other community facilities
- ❏ Help students and caregivers to increase the resources within their own communities because poverty is a matter of lack of resources

In the Hallways and Within the School, I Will

- ❏ Make good nutrition a priority
- ❏ Emphasize good hydration for learning
- ❏ Examine curriculum and books for examples of bias and work toward a plan for eliminating bias throughout the school
- ❏ Set norms that include the respect for all people
- ❏ Set norms that say quality learning is essential for all children
- ❏ Provide advisory groups that include students as well as community people
- ❏ Provide opportunities for afterschool activities
- ❏ Provide opportunities for additional resources that are a part of the school budget, such as nurses, counselors, and librarians
- ❏ Make sure that the resources in my school are rich in culture and reflect the cultures of my students. While Martin Luther King Day is important, it should not be the only time of the year that we celebrate diversity
- ❏ Be aware of students who are absent too much, in danger of dropping out, or in danger of failure
- ❏ Provide an adult advocate for every student in the school, which can be done through teams of teachers and senior students
- ❏ Fight for better conditions for my school if they are not up to par with other schools in my region
- ❏ Be proactive in asking for the resources that my students need to be successful

(Continued)

Form 6.1 (Continued)

❏ Provide ongoing professional development that includes ways to reach students in my school and that examines the best practices, especially in regard to brain research and learning

❏ Understand how to modify best practices for culture and poverty

In the Classroom, I Will

❏ Set classroom standards that define expectations that all students will be respected

❏ Bond with all of the students first before providing substance

❏ Model the behavior that I expect of my students

❏ Lead my students to the resources available to them

❏ Make my students aware of the need for good nutrition and hydration in regard to learning

❏ Communicate caring and concern for all students

❏ Communicate high expectations while keeping the threat level low

❏ Help students to understand how their own brains work and how that affects all that they do

❏ Build positive self-efficacy in my students

❏ Teach the "hidden" rules to students and when they are used

❏ Build positive self-esteem in my students

❏ Provide a variety of teaching resources in the classroom that take into account the backgrounds, ethnicity, and culture of my students

❏ Use a variety of modalities in the classroom, especially visual and kinesthetic

❏ Contextualize the lessons

❏ Create experiences that help students make connections between prior learning and experiences and the new learning

❏ Create opportunities for students to set personal goals for the learning

- ❑ Explicitly show students how to use self-talk and other techniques to revise their goals when they encounter problems
- ❑ Help students to complete work at a quality level by directly teaching goal setting
- ❑ Provide specific and prescriptive feedback on an ongoing basis to students
- ❑ Teach in a variety of modalities so that students learn in the way that they are accustomed
- ❑ Help students to make the transition from the language of the street to the language of the classroom
- ❑ Provide opportunities for students to work together in heterogeneous groups
- ❑ Emphasize the gifts that all students bring to the table
- ❑ Resist the philosophy that students from poverty are children who need to be "fixed"
- ❑ Recognize and overcome linguistic bias
- ❑ Recognize and overcome stereotyping bias
- ❑ Recognize and overcome exclusion bias
- ❑ Recognize and overcome fragmentation/isolation bias
- ❑ Recognize and overcome selectivity bias
- ❑ Recognize and overcome unreality bias

Vocabulary Summary

BIAS

Bias is belief that something or someone is inferior or superior based on a set of criteria.

CLASSROOM CLIMATE

Classroom climate refers to two major areas within the classroom:

1. The physical makeup of the classroom, such as lighting, color of the room, smell of the room, seating arrangement, visuals, and temperature.

2. The emotional mood of the classroom, such as how students feel about the learning, the teacher, the other members of the classroom, and the positive as well as negative emotions within the class.

DIRECT INSTRUCTION

Direct instruction is instructional delivery primarily from the teacher that encourages a high level of learner engagement and requires structured, accomplishable tasks.

Under direct instruction, the teacher might follow these steps:

1. Introduce the topic and the vocabulary necessary to understand the topic

2. Model, demonstrate, or discuss the information

3. Provide opportunities for students to practice the learning in a very structured environment with the teacher providing feedback

4. Provide opportunities for students to work independently using the new information

DIVERSITY

Diversity refers to the ways in which we differ from each other, including gender, age, ethnicity, culture, religion, exceptionality, and socioeconomic status.

DUAL CULTURE

Students from fringe cultures have to adapt to their true culture and obey the rules of the dominant culture in order to be successful in the classroom and workplace. This often brings about added conflicts.

ENGLISH LANGUAGE LEARNERS

English language learners are students whose primary language is something other than English and who have a limited knowledge of the English language. Because students who do not know the words cannot activate the semantic memory system (which stores words), it is important that teachers activate other memory systems by using visuals and movement. We also include in this category those students who speak the language of the streets, a dialect or who speak Ebonics as a primary language with peers.

ETHNIC IDENTITY

Ethnic identity refers to our identity in a group in which we have a common culture based on language, history, geography, and often physical characteristics.

ETHNOCENTRISM

Ethnocentrism is the belief that one's own ethnicity is superior to others.

EXCEPTIONALITY

The term *exceptionality* refers to the characteristics that make us different, such as handicapping conditions or giftedness.

HIDDEN RULES OF SOCIETY

According to Payne (2001), every social class has *hidden* rules that are only known to that class. For example, for children from poverty, the most important possession is people: for the middle class, it is things, and for the wealthy it is one-of-a-kind objects, legacies, or pedigrees. Money for those in poverty is to be spent; for the middle class, it is to be managed; and for those from wealth, it is to be invested. Where one went to school distinguishes the social rich from the merely rich and those below. In terms of time, those in poverty live for the moment, the middle class look to the future, and the wealthy believe in traditions and history. It is interesting to note that each class believes that everyone knows their hidden rules, but the truth is that we tend to know the rules of our group only.

INSTRUCTIONAL CASUALTIES

Instructional casualties is a term that is associated with legislation in Elementary and Secondary Education Act (ESEA) of 2004, which calls into question why so many minorities and students from poverty are placed in special education. The question is often whether they were correctly placed or if their struggles in school are due to a system that does not take into account how they learn and the hidden bias within tests and curriculum. Add to that instructional personnel who have not been provided with the knowledge and skills to modify for culture and poverty.

INTRINSIC MOTIVATION

Intrinsic motivation is internal motivation associated with activities that are rewarding in themselves. An example of intrinsic motivation would be a student who reads a book because he or she wants to learn more about the subject or character or because the student loves to read.

Some researchers believe that the frequent use of rewards in classrooms is a deterrent to intrinsic motivation.

LEARNING ENVIRONMENT

The *learning environment* comprises the mood, tone, and physical conditions that surround the learning.

LOCUS OF CONTROL

According to McCune, Stephens, and Lowe (1999), *locus of control* refers to the degree to which students feel that events they experience are under their own control (inner control) rather than under the control of other people or forces outside of themselves (external control). Researchers believe that students will be more likely to engage in learning activities when they attribute success or failure to things they can control like their own effort, or lack of it, rather than to forces over which they have little or no control, such as their ability, luck, or outside forces. Teachers should help students, especially at-risk learners, link their successes to something they did to contribute to the success. When this occurs, the students develop self-efficacy and the confidence that they have the power within themselves to be successful.

MELTING-POT THEORY

The *melting-pot theory* was the belief popular in the United States for many years that those who come to this country should assimilate and blend into the dominant culture. Most Americans have come to believe that we need to embrace cultural differences rather than try to make everyone like us.

MINORITY GROUP

A *minority group* is a racial or ethnic group that has the least number within a society.

MODALITY

Modality is the way in which students take in information. The three common modalities:

1. *Visual.* Visual students need to see the material, and, in math, they need to see how the math works. Simply telling them the material is not enough. The largest number of students in the classroom are in this group. Could we raise math scores across the country if we could find more ways to show students how math works?

2. *Auditory.* Auditory students want to hear the new information. They usually like to listen and take notes. The smallest number of students in the classroom is in this group.

3. *Kinesthetic.* Kinesthetic students need hand-on experiences. They also need movement or you will lose their interest and they may become discipline problems.

MOTIVATION

Motivation is the willingness or drive to accomplish something. It may be extrinsic (driven by outside forces, such as the promise of a reward) or intrinsic (driven from within).

MULTICULTURAL EDUCATION

Multicultural education is a process designed to increase awareness and acceptance among people of different cultures.

NONDISCRIMINATORY TESTING

Nondiscriminatory testing is testing that takes into account a student's cultural and linguistic background.

PERSONAL FABLE

Personal fable refers to the belief that "my life is different from everyone else's, so no one can understand how I feel or think." This view of life may result in either a feeling of isolation (usually predicated by a changing body) or a willingness to engage in risky behaviors, such as the belief that "others get pregnant, but it won't happen to me."

RESIDENTIAL SEGREGATION

Residential segregation occurs when the majority race moves to newer and more affluent areas of the cities and towns, leaving the poor in often rundown and less desirable neighborhoods.

RESPONSE TO INTERVENTION

Response to intervention is a process born out of the changes to ESEA in 2004 that call for all teachers and staff to recognize and intervene at the first point of struggling in school. The model follows a model coming from the medical community that says early intervention will correct mild and short-term problems for 85% of the student population, 15% will need additional interventions at a more intense level and 5% will probably need the services of special education programs. Schools create their own models based on the regulations from ESEA 2004 and No Child Left Behind.

SELF-CONCEPT

Self-concept refers to the way in which an individual sees himself or herself.

SELF-EFFICACY

Self-efficacy is the self-confidence to be successful based on past experiences. It is stronger than self-esteem because it is built on fact rather than "I think and I feel." According to Dwyer & Cummings (2001), self-efficacy is the belief that you have the power to accomplish a given task and will determine whether a student attempts the task or avoids it. Cummings goes on to say that self-efficacy can be instilled in students when teachers do the following:

- Teach goal setting
- Encourage positive self-talk
- Break long-term projects into small steps
- Measure the success of each small step

- Involve students in the self-evaluation of their effort
- Provide opportunities to be successful without watering down the curriculum

SELF-ESTEEM

Self-esteem is the value a person sets on his or her self-worth.

SELF-FULFILLING PROPHECY

A *self-fulfilling prophecy* occurs when one's biased beliefs about what should occur will influence the results to confirm one's expectations.

Researchers over time such as Good and Brophy (1966), Marzano (2001), and Williams (2003) provide the following examples of how teachers often treat students based on their perception of them. Teachers may

- Seat high achievers across from and down the middle of the room
- Seat low achievers far from the teacher
- Seat low achievers near each other in a group
- Give fewer nonverbal cues to low achievers during instruction, such as smile less often or maintain less eye contact
- Call on high achievers much more frequently than on low achievers
- Use a longer wait time for responses from high achievers
- Fail to stay with low achievers when they attempt a response
- Criticize low achievers more frequently for incorrect responses
- Praise low achievers more frequently for inadequate public responses
- Provide low achievers with less frequent and less specific feedback regarding their responses
- Demand less work and effort from low achievers
- Interrupt performance of low achievers more frequently
- Talk negatively about low achievers more frequently
- Punish off-task behavior of low achievers and more frequently ignore it in high achievers

SOCIOECONOMIC STATUS

Socioeconomic status is the relationship of an individual's economic status to social factors, including education, occupation, and place of residence.

VOICES

According to Payne (2001), we all have three *voices* that we use throughout our lives: *the child voice, the parent voice,* and *the adult voice.*

The child voice has the following attributes: It is defensive, victimized, emotional, whining, strongly negative, nonverbal, and has a losing attitude. It may also be playful and spontaneous.

Example: "Quit picking on me."

The parent voice tends to be authoritative, directive, judgmental, evaluative, demanding, punitive, sometimes threatening, and has a win-lose attitude. It can also be loving and supportive.

Example: "You do as I say."

The adult voice tends to be nonjudgmental, free of negatives, factual, and often speaks in a question format. It has a win-win attitude.

Example: "In what ways could this be resolved?"

Using the parent voice with children from poverty often causes the situation to become more heated. Payne (2001) says to use the adult voice and to begin to teach children from poverty how to use that voice beginning in about the fourth grade. Payne calls the adult voice the "language of negotiation." It is the voice most used in business and in the school setting, and it should be taught to children from poverty to help them to be successful in those worlds.

Vocabulary
Posttest

At the beginning of this book, you were given a vocabulary list and a pretest on that vocabulary. Below are the posttest and the answer key for the vocabulary assessment.

Instructions: For each question given, choose the best answer or answers. More than one answer may be correct.

1. The belief that one culture is superior to other groups is called . . .

    A. The melting-pot theory
    B. Ethnocentrism
    C. Exceptionality
    D. Diversity

2. Diane Madden is a teacher at East Middle School, where she teaches eighth-grade English. Ms. Madden talked with teachers from the seventh grade prior to the beginning of school and asked them to give her their opinion about the students she will be teaching this year. Several of the teachers said that she shouldn't even try to teach "those" students the classics because they will not understand them. This advice is what type of bias?

    A. Linguistic
    B. Exclusion

C. Persuasive

D. Stereotyping

3. Students who come from poverty are usually not . . .

___A. Kinesthetic learners

B. Visual learners

C. Auditory learners

___D. Declarative learners

B, C

4. Students who believe that they just have bad luck in school may be suffering from poor . . .

A. Diversity

B. Locus of control

C. Self-efficacy

D. Self-esteem

B, C, D

5. Students who believe that they can succeed because they have succeeded in the past are practicing . . .

A. The auditory modality

B. Locus of control

C. Self-efficacy

D. Extrinsic motivation

C only

6. Teachers who tell students that they will get candy for good work are using . . .

A. Locus of control –

B. Intrinsic motivation

___C. Self-fulfilling prophecy

D. Extrinsic motivation

D only

7. Which of the following is not true of response to intervention?

A. It is a part of the 2004 amendments to Elementary and Secondary Education Act (ESEA)

B. It is the responsibility of regular education teachers as well as special education

C. It allows students to be placed in special education if the learning difficulty is caused by poverty

    D. It requires interventions before a student shows failure

8. Students who have lived in situations of great stress over time often experience . . .

    A. Imaginary audience

    _B. Self-fulfilling prophecy

    _C. Exceptionality

    —D. Learned helplessness

D only

9. Teachers who teach in a variety of formats so that they teach to all races and ethnicities are practicing . . .

    A. Contextualization

    B. Ethnocentrism

    C. Pluralism

    D. Indirect teaching

A + C

10. English language learners (ELLs) . . .

    A. Are considered as having low socioeconomic status

    B. Speak a language other than English as their primary language

    C. Are often shy in class

    D. Have low intrinsic motivation to learn

11. Raul is in Mr. Vasquez's math class at Moors Middle School. Raul is struggling because he cannot grasp some of the math concepts being taught. Mr. Vasquez has added graphic organizers to help students like Raul learn more successfully. Raul is probably what kind of learner?

    A. Kinesthetic

    B. Visual

    C. Auditory

    D. Dual skill

12. Which of the following are used to determine at-risk students?

+ (C)

    A. Low socioeconomic status

    B. ELL status

C. Previous failure

D. Ethnicity

13. Marty came to school on Friday with red streaks in his hair (just like his two best friends). Marty is exhibiting . . .

___ A. Personal fable

___ B. Self-efficacy   c only

C. Imaginary audience

— D. Self-fulfilling prophecy

14. When students become what we expect them to become, it is called . . .

A. An imaginary audience

___ B. A self-fulfilling prophecy   B

___ C. Self-efficacy الشخص

D. Personal fable ~ الشخص

15. Most students in the classroom are which type of learners?

A. Auditory

B. Visual   B only

C. Kinesthetic

D. Intrinsic

16. *Diversity* means . . .

A. Differences

B. Ethnicity   A only

C. Exceptionality

D. Bias

17. The belief that people moving to this country should become like us is called . . .

A. Exceptionality

B. Ethnocentrism   only D

C. Multicultural

D. The melting-pot theory

18. Intrinsic motivation is triggered by . . .

A. Relevance

+ A   B. Stickers

    C. Emotions
    D. Relationships

19. Kelvin Waters has difficulty completing tasks once he begins. Research on which topic would be most helpful for him?

    A. The metacognitive system
    B. The self-system
    C. The cognitive system
    D. The procedural system

20. Which of the following is part of classroom climate?

    A. The lighting in the room
    B. The amount of tension in the room
    C. The way the room smells
    D. The socioeconomic status of the students

Vocabulary Pretest and Posttest Answer Key

1. B	11. B
2. D	12. A, B, C
3. B, C	13. C
4. B, C, D	14. B
5. C	15. B
6. D	16. A
7. C	17. D
8. D	18. A, C, D
9. A, C	19. A
10. B, C	20. A, B, C

References

Arroyo, C. (January, 2008). *The funding gap.* Washington, DC: Education Trust.

Bartelt, D. W. (1994). The macro ecology of educational outcomes. *School-Community Connections, 3*(1), 2–3.

Benard, B. (2003). Turnaround teachers and schools. In B. Williams (Ed.), *Closing the achievement gap; A vision for changing beliefs and practices* (2nd ed., pp. 115–137). Alexandria, VA: ASCD.

Brown University. (2007). *The diversity kit: An introductory resource for social change in education (Part I: Culture).* Providence, RI: Northeast and Islands Regional Educational Laboratory at Brown University (LAB).

Covey, S. R. (1989). *Seven habits of highly effective people.* New York: Simon & Schuster.

Cozzens, L. (1998) Watson.org Retrieved February 15, 2008, from http:// www.watson.org/~lisa/blackhistory/early-civilrights/brown.html

Doidge, N. (2006). *The brain that changes itself: Stories of personal triumph from the frontiers of brain science.* New York: Viking Penguin. (See p. 24)

Dwyer, A.L., & Cummings, A.L. (2001). Stress, self-efficacy, social support, and coping strategies in university students. *Canadian Journal of Counseling 35* (3), 208–212.

Education Trust. (2007). *The Funding Gap.* Retrieved on March 14, 2008, from www2.edtrust.org/EdTrust/Press+Room/funding gap)7.htm

Garcia, E. (1994). *Understanding and meeting the challenge of student cultural diversity.* Boston: Houghton Mifflin.

Geertz, C. (1973). *The interpretation of cultures.* New York: Basic Books.

Gibbs, J. (1994). *Tribes.* Santa Rosa, CA: Center Source.

Good, T. L., & Brophy, J. E. (1996). *Looking in classrooms* (3rd ed.). New York: Harper & Row.

Greenberg, E. (with Weber, K.). (2008). *Generation we: How millennial youth are taking over America and changing our world forever.* Emeryville, CA: Pachatusan.

Heller, K., Holtzman, W., & Messick, S. (1982). *Placing children in special education: A strategy for equity.* Washington, DC: National Academy of Science Press.

Hosp, J. L. (2009). *Response to intervention and the disproportionate representation of culturally and linguistically diverse students in special education.* Retrieved April 7, 2009, from www.rtinetwork.org/Learn/Diversity/ar/DisproportionateRepresentation

Jensen, E. (1997). *Completing the puzzle: The brain-compatible approach to learning.* Del Mar, CA: Brain Stone.

Jensen, E. (1998). *Introduction to brain-compatible learning.* Del Mar, CA: Brain Stone.

Jensen, E. (2006). *Enriching the brain: How to maximize every learner's potential.* San Francisco, CA: Jossey-Bass.

Jensen, E. (2010). *Different brains, different learners: How to reach the hard to reach.* Thousand Oaks, CA: Corwin.

Johnson, R. T., Johnson, D. W., & Holubec, E. J. (1994). *Cooperative learning in the classroom.* Alexandria, VA: ASCD.

Karoly, L. (2007, November 8). Studies examine California's school readiness. Retrieved April 11, 2008, from www.RAND/news releases/Studies Examine California's School Readiness

Kotulak, R. (1996). *Inside the brain.* Kansas City, MO: Andrews McMeel.

Lindsey, R. B., Robbins, K. N., & Terrell, R. D. (2009). *Cultural proficiency: A manual for school leaders.* Thousand Oaks, CA: Corwin.

Mangaliman, J. (2007). Poverty can't explain racial, ethnic divide. *Mercury News.* Retrieved on August 6, 2007, from mercury news.com

Manning, J. B., & Kovach, J. A. (2003). The continuing challenges of excellence and equity. In B. Williams *Closing the achievement gap: A vision for changing beliefs and practices* (2nd ed., pp. 25–47). Alexandria, VA: ASCD.

Marzano, R. J. (1998). *A theory based meta-analysis of research on instruction.* Aurora, CO: McREL.

Marzano, R. J. (2001). *Designing a new taxonomy of educational objectives.* Thousand Oaks, CA: Corwin.

Marzano, R. J., & Kendall, J. S. (2008). *Designing and assessing educational objectives: Applying the new taxonomy.* Thousand Oaks, CA: Corwin.

Marzano, R. J., Pickering, D. J., & Pollock, J. E. (2001). *Classroom instruction that works.* Alexandria, VA: ASCD.

McCune, S. L., Stephens, D. E., & Lowe, M. E. (1999). *Barron's how to prepare for the ExCET* (2nd ed.). Hauppauge, NY: Barron's.

McKinney, S., Flenner, C., Frazier, W., & Abrams, L. (2006) Responding to the needs of at-risk students in poverty. Retrieved September 15, 2007, from www.usca.edu/essays/V01172006/mckinney.pdf

National Association of Secondary School Principals. (1996). *Breaking ranks: Changing an American institution.* Reston, VA: Author.

Payne, R. K. (2001) *A framework for understanding poverty.* Highlands, TX: Aha! Process.

Pink, D. (2007). *A whole new mind: Moving from the information age to the conceptual age.* New York: Riverhead Books.

Sousa, D. (1995). *How the brain learns.* Reston, VA: National Association of Secondary School Principals.

Sprenger, M. (2002). *Becoming a wiz at brain-based teaching: How to make every year your best year.* Thousand Oaks, CA: Corwin.

Tileston, D. W. (2000). *Ten best teaching practices: How brain research, learning styles, and standards define teaching competencies.* Thousand Oaks, CA: Corwin.

Tileston, D. W. (2004a). *What every teacher should know about effective teaching strategies.* Thousand Oaks, CA: Corwin.

Tileston, D. W. (2004b). *What every teacher should know about student assessment.* Thousand Oaks, CA: Corwin.

Tileston, D. W., & Darling, S. K. (2009). *Closing the poverty and culture gap: Strategies to reach every student.* Thousand Oaks, CA: Corwin.

U.S. Department of Education. (2001). *No Child Left Behind.* Retrieved February 23, 2010, from http://www2.ed.gov/nclb/landing.jhtml

U.S. Department of Education. (2004). *Individuals with Disabilities in Education Act.* Retrieved February 23, 2010, from http://idea.ed.gov/

Wang, M. C., & Kovach, J. A. (1996). Bridging the achievement gap in urban schools: Reducing educational segregation and advancing resilience-promoting strategies. In B. Williams (Ed.), *Closing the achievement gap* (pp. 10–36). Alexandria, VA: ASCD.

Whistler, N., & Williams, J. (1990). *Literature and cooperative learning: Pathway to literacy.* Sacramento, CA: Literature Co-Op.

Williams, B. (1996). A social vision for urban education: Focused, comprehensive, and integrated change. In B. Williams (Ed.), *Closing the achievement gap* (pp. 148–160). Alexandria, VA: ASCD.

Williams, B. (2003). *Closing the achievement gap: A vision for changing beliefs and practices* (2nd ed.). Alexandria, VA: ASCD.

Yancey, W., & Saporito, S. (1994). *Urban schools and neighborhoods: A handbook for building an ecological database* [Research report]. Philadelphia: Office of Educational Research and Improvement, National Center on Education in the Inner Cities, Temple University Center for Research in Human Development and Education.

Zeichner, K. M. (2003). Educating teachers to close the achievement gap: Issues of pedagogy, knowledge, and teacher preparation. In B. Williams (Ed.), *Closing the achievement gap* (2nd ed., pp. 99–114). Alexandria, VA: ASCD.

Zhoa, Y. (2009). *Catching up or leading the way: American eduction in the age of globalization.* Alexandria, VA: ASCD.

Index

CORWIN

A SAGE Company

The Corwin logo—a raven striding across an open book—represents the union of courage and learning. Corwin is committed to improving education for all learners by publishing books and other professional development resources for those serving the field of PreK–12 education. By providing practical, hands-on materials, Corwin continues to carry out the promise of its motto: **"Helping Educators Do Their Work Better."**